AF379400

Athena to Barbie

Athena *to* Barbie

BODIES, ARCHETYPES, AND WOMEN'S SEARCH FOR SELF

J. Lenore Wright

Fortress Press
Minneapolis

ATHENA TO BARBIE
Bodies, Archetypes, and Women's Search for Self

Scripture quotations are from the New Revised Standard Version Bible, copyright © 1989 National Council of the Churches of Christ in the United States of America. Used by permission. All rights reserved worldwide.

Cover art: Untitled oil painting by Sara D. Cocke Wright. Reprinted with permission by the owner.
Cover design: Savanah Landerholm

Print ISBN: 978-1-5064-8047-3
eBook ISBN: 978-1-5064-8048-0

Contents

Preface   vii

Introduction   1

1   Delivering Mary:
    Womb as Sacred Space   11

2   Conquering Athena:
    Womb as Political Space   35

3   Subduing Venus:
    Womb as Erotic Space   67

4   Playing Barbie:
    Womb as Material Space   93

Conclusion   121

Notes   139
Bibliography   179
Index   187

Preface

I conceived this book while writing a journal article about pregnancy loss. The essay was meant to shed light on the grief expectant parents experience after miscarriage. I employed the usual academic tools, from literature review to final edits. Done. And not done. Not really. And, as it turns out, probably not ever. I know intimately the physical and emotional wreckage that accompanies pregnancy loss. I also know that 15–20 percent of pregnancies end in miscarriage. I have learned that partners grieve lost pregnancies, my husband, Henry, included. What started as a purely academic endeavor—a phenomenology of miscarriage—became, philosophically speaking, self-involved. Writing about miscarriage opened up the psychic space where I (perhaps we) store the defining fixtures of life's emotional landscape: loss, rejection, and trauma as well as achievement, acceptance, and resolution. This book was born out of a single academic project, a collection of personal experiences, and an ongoing exploration of women's search for self.

Athena to Barbie exposes and honors women's bodily and psychic markings. I trace the search for identity *with a womb and female form* in a world that tells women who they are *because of* their reproductive roles and bodily parts. The real work of the womb (from the negative moment of women's historic oppression toward the positive potential of a better future) and the real work of feminist philosophy (from an identification with woman's Otherness toward a resistance to sexist norms) requires an unraveling of the logic of womanhood. We must reconsider historic sources of self and establish generative understandings of what and who we are. Experiencing oneself as a woman demands a confrontation with the womb.

Archetypal ideals weigh heavily in women's search for self. Female archetypes produce idealized standards of womanhood that discipline the body and shape the mind. Archetypal ideals also weigh heavily in religion, politics, society, economics, and ultimately, in the status of women themselves. *Athena to Barbie* surveys four female archetypes that inform women's identity. Collective archetypal material—from imagery, inferences, and reception—directs women's navigation of life in a presumptively reproductive body. Archetypes also influence how women exercise the agency and authority vested in the womb. I appeal to Simone de Beauvoir as I consider reproductive (and nonreproductive) female bodies—*women are their bodies in a way that men are not.* Her account of female alienation and subordination in *The Second Sex*, along with her articulation, new at the time, of a woman's loss of personal and social identity, coheres with feelings of failure, isolation, and malformation women associate with female embodiment. I draw on Virginia Woolf, who theorizes women's inability to articulate female experiences in *A Room of One's Own—women lack a language of their own because they have had too little education, privacy, and subsistence to form female literary traditions.* Speaking about pregnancy and miscarriage from a philosophical perspective is practically inconceivable. More than 80 percent of academic philosophers are men; the life and language of philosophy are predisposed to male experiences of reality, experiences often formulated as universal truths. I deploy the radical Jewish feminist philosopher Andrea Dworkin, feminism's Old Testament prophet who cries out in the wilderness of female oppression. I am compelled by her argument that intercourse has a political meaning—that female subordination is inextricably bound up with the use of women's bodies for sexual gratification and, either intentionally or accidentally, reproduction. *Intercourse is a key to women's lower human status.* Beauvoir, Woolf, and Dworkin represent different streams of feminist thought. But they share a critical concern for the meaning, role, and value of female bodies and wombs. For women to become fully agential subjects—persons who exercise self-determination, enjoy self-respect, command authority, and exhibit integrity—intercourse, pregnancy, and childbirth must undergo philosophical examination.

My analysis develops out of productive counterpoints that elevate the body without predefining its meaning. Jack Halberstam, Luce Irigaray, Julia Kristeva, Amy Mullin, Kelly Oliver, Adrienne Rich, Sissel Undheim, Cynthia Willett, and Iris Marion Young treat embodiment as a site of resistance to rather than complicity with bodily control. Their positions on gendered subjectivity include the claim that pregnancy is (or can be) a creative and expansive experience rather than a reductive and disempowering act. Many helpfully problematize the female condition without erasing the feminine body entirely. They refine the question of womanhood—from trans-womanhood to cis-womanhood—and make space for persons who exemplify new performances of woman, performances that overlap, parallel, and intersect one another.

Archetypal bodies and the various meanings of pregnancy they signify can serve as a powerful heuristic for living as a woman. Retheorizing pregnancy can create new understandings of embodiment and contest established meanings of femininity. Reimagining womanhood and recontextualizing archetypal knowledge can yield positive readings of the pregnant subject by encompassing both the realization that women have suffered oppression vis-à-vis pregnancy and the hope that women can recast pregnancy as an empowering experience. Assigning positive value to female bodies and the labor they perform helps disclose the forces that diminish women's lives and push back against them. Pregnancy can serve as a site of feminist resistance to oppression, enable a reclamation of female freedom, and expand the experience of becoming a woman. All women, whether or not they are mothers, must negotiate the womb.

I am especially grateful to many strong women who have supported this project. Heidi Bostic deserves heaps of praise for reading multiple versions of the manuscript. Her always incisive insights shored up gaps in my analysis and challenged my thinking in all the best ways. She cheered me on during bouts of exhaustion, refusing to let me quit. She and her spouse, Stephen Pluháček, a gifted philosopher and interlocutor, have supported and enriched my work immensely. Heidi and Steve make life richer. Anne-Marie Schultz, my philosophical muse and treasured friend, has been fiercely dedicated to my work. She enabled my progress by advocating for course releases and sabbatical support. She also read and shaped early chapters of the book and spurred me on through encouraging texts, emails, and phone calls. Anne's generosity and tenacity have enhanced my life, elevated my work, and expanded my academic interests. I cherish our conversations and shared experiences as female philosophers. My Women Faculty Writing Program cohort, led by Lisa Shaver, Kara Poe Alexander, and Julie Holcomb, has been exceptionally supportive. Drafts of the book were completed during our dedicated writing time every Friday afternoon. Other women academics—women leaders at Baylor University, former and current colleagues in the Baylor Interdisciplinary Core (BIC), and friends at other institutions—have inspired my work in direct and indirect ways. I am especially grateful for the support and parallel efforts of Mary Atwell, Robyn Driskell, Beverly Gaventa, Danielle Tumminio Hansen, Mandy McMichael, Jacqueline-Bethel Mougoué, Anne Lewis Osler, and Sarah Walden. They question the unquestioned, marginal position of women in history and culture. Their scholarly pursuits have emboldened me to take up subjects dismissed, even ridiculed, by mainstream philosophers. I gladly join them in exploring the crimped edges of female identity. Many former women students are present in this work as well. Conversations with Skye Perryman, Aya Farhat, Adina Kelley, Hilary Yancey, Teresa Dean, and Angelica Mazé have caused me to confront my philosophical commitments and rethink gender identity in broader terms. I thank them for making me a better person and teacher.

Many male supporters and allies deserve special recognition too. My "new faculty orientation" friends Andy Arterbury and Doug Weaver have been anchors throughout my academic journey and, with respect to this project, provided remarkable help with chapter 1. Their commitment to women's equality has inspired nearly two decades of honest conversations. I am immensely grateful for our friendship of the good, to borrow Aristotle's term. I also thank Karl Aho, Paul Carron, Jesse Jordan, Chuck McDaniel, and Mike Whitenton, former and current members of my BIC Writing Group, for their generous spirits and good minds. My BIC colleague Sam Perry supplied reassuring notes during many weekend writing marathons. He buoyed my spirits with music recommendations too. Joshua Smith served as an exceptional research assistant early in the project. Former mentees and teaching assistants Aaron Ellis, John Garza, Yunus Prasetya, and John Rosenbaum have been superb conversationalists and co-teachers. Finally, I am steadfastly grateful to progressive male thinkers who set the stage for women's success at Baylor and played pivotal roles in my professional development. Bob Baird, Bill Bellinger, Ray Cannon, Tom Hanks, David Longfellow, and the late Carl Vaught are foremost among them. I cherish them all.

I am grateful to Baylor University and the Honors College for a semester research leave, without which this book would never have materialized. I owe a special thank-you to my administrative colleagues in the Academy for Teaching and Learning (ATL), Craig Clarkson and Christopher Richmann. Craig's exemplary management of the ATL erased my concerns about devoting time to this project. His engagement with the book's central argument—and playful encouragement of my feminist side—fostered delightful, intellectual exchange. Christopher's steady hand at the tiller, advancing the work of the ATL each and every day, aptly kept the ATL afloat. Finally, there cannot exist more winsome, supportive colleagues than Lyndsay DiPietro and Austin Smith, who pulled extra ATL duty to make the book possible. I am honored to serve alongside these four stellar human beings. I owe another special thank-you to Leslie Ballard, who is nothing short of a miracle worker. Les tackled the difficult task of putting this book together by tracking down references, formatting citations, and preparing bibliographic information. His steady pace of productivity helped me stick to my established timeline. I also wish to acknowledge the outside readers for Fortress Press who took time to offer invaluable comments on the manuscript draft.

Carey Newman is a superb editor in every sense of the term. He understands good writing and directs ideas toward productive ends. He also possesses an exhaustive knowledge of the publishing world, though his investment in books never eclipses his investment in the writers who produce them. Carey grasped *Athena to Barbie* right away and believed in the book from the first sketchy outline to the final footnote. He has been an exemplary advocate and sounding board. I cannot thank him enough for his energy, encouragement, and insights. It has been an honor to work with him and the team of professionals at Fortress Press. I have enjoyed more than one lighthearted exchange with Esther Diley and Elvis Ramirez.

I am incapable of adequately expressing my praise and gratitude for Henry Wright. He rolled up his sleeves again to support me, from taking our children on day trips so that I could write to securing copyright permissions for the book images. He graciously indulged conversations about each chapter and offered perceptive input. Everyone should have at least one person who believes in them more than they believe in themselves. Henry is my person. We fell in love over (and with) philosophy. I have stayed nestled in the world of ideas while he has mastered other professional domains, the world of law among them. Despite his array of accomplishments, he still delights in a keen philosophical conversation, eager to return time and again to a subject he loves. I dedicate *Athena to Barbie* to Henry William Wright II and our beloved children, Henry Wallace Wright II (H. W.) and Carl Haze Wright.

Introduction

But, you may say, *this is a book about womanhood. It is a story of female identity and women's deeply mythic sources of self-knowing. What has that got to do with the womb? I will try to explain.*[1] A pregnant subject on a throne, that classical symbol of authority, sanctioning woman as mother. Her foot atop a marker identifying interior anatomical structures. Her nude body on display. Her abdominal cavity opened to expose a fetus inside. She is neither immobile nor moving. She balances herself on the edge of her seat, unaware of the figures who gaze at her from above. She is oblivious to us, her immediate viewers. She is also blind to the generations of medical students who studied her from the pages of a textbook for which Charles Estienne made her. The image's urban setting, with its visual references to scientific and technological advances, reflects the growth of the city in the sixteenth and seventeenth centuries. Yet as her representation makes clear, a woman's contribution to civic life lies in reproduction. Her role is to populate the city, a role that neither individuates her as a human being nor distinguishes her from other women. She lacks any sign of self-awareness, any indication of a rational capacity. She is a reproductive creature.

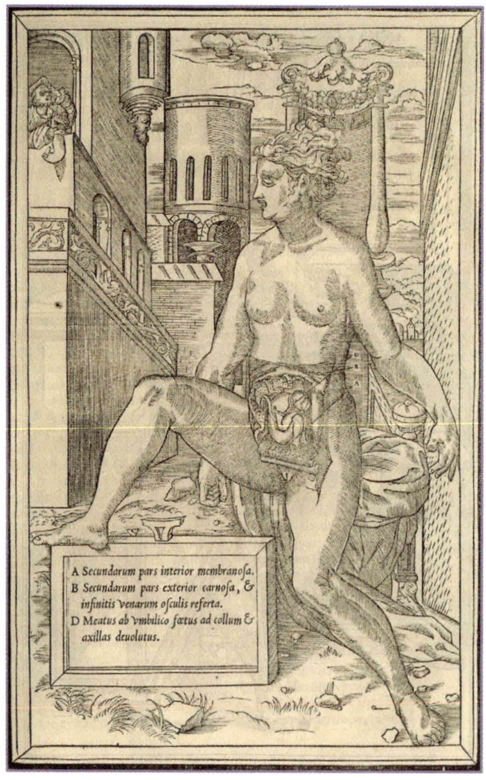

Charles Estienne (ca. 1504–1564) [author]. Étienne de la Rivière (d. 1569) [anatomist]. *De dissection partium corporis humani libri tres.* Paris, 1545. Woodcut. National Library of Medicine, U.S.A.

By contrast, the figure in a 1773 mezzotint by Jacques Fabien Gautier d'Agoty tells a different story. She is a particular rather than an archetypal woman, a woman who appears to experience pregnancy as a knowing subject. Her face bears a stoic, Roman quality in keeping with the neoclassical elements of late eighteenth-century art. She crosses her arms over her skinned body—she is, unlike Estienne's figure, flayed from the neck down—and coyly eyes her audience, playfully acknowledging their gaze. She communicates an understanding of her role in anatomical study and

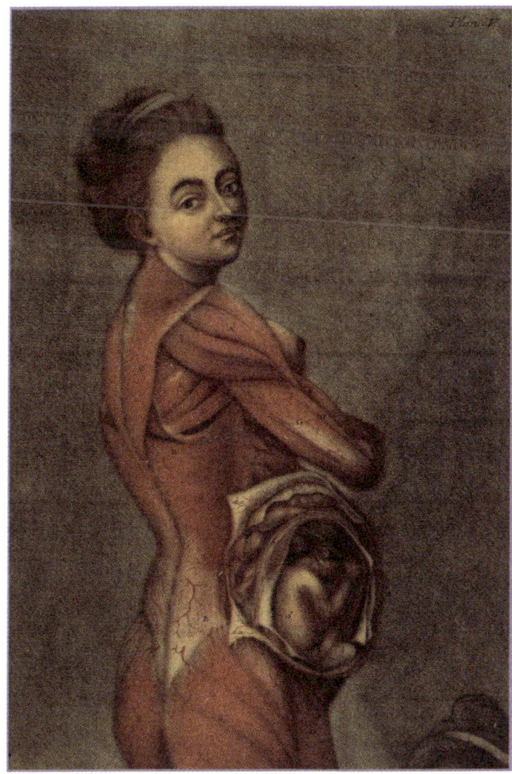

Jacques Fabien Gautier d'Agoty, *Anatomie des parties de la génértion de l'homme et de la femme* (1773), National Library of Medicine, U.S.A.

consciously participates in the unveiling of her uterine wall. She is, to use the literary idiom, "enlivened," offering a notable counterpoint to the docility Estienne equates with pregnancy. Her living subjectivity redraws the line between life and death, portraying an impossible condition for the sake of medical understanding. Her paradoxical depiction of lived experience invites a rich reading of the pregnant subject.

The question that opens this book—the question of womanhood and the womb—takes the form of the opening query of Virginia Woolf's *A Room of One's Own*. Woolf situates her exploration of woman's nature in the context of literature. She wonders aloud, addressing an unseen audience, what women and fiction have to do with a room of one's own. She offers a partial conclusion—"a woman must have money and a room of her own if she is to write fiction"—before she advances an analysis of womanhood as such.[2] *Athena to Barbie* resituates the Woolfian exploration of woman in the context of the wombed body.

Wombs and woman signify one another. Neither progressive politics nor postmodern critiques has undone their conceptual co-mingling. One cannot easily disentangle woman from womb given the regressive mood of the historical moment and—perhaps more so—because of our cultural (and deeply internalized) attachments to wombs and what they represent. In truth, the concept of "womb" teems with meaning that transcends person, time, and place yet also shapes women's lived, bodily realities.

Wombs are not uteruses. Conceived as carriers of life, wombs contain and nurture life while the uterus may be empty—of a fetus as well as connotations of care. The womb is posited as woman's essence, her true nature. It is the perceived locus of female power. Because nature circumscribes identity, *what* women are (reproductive beings) defines *who* women are: nurturers and caregivers. Female identity is therefore tied to a wombed, nurturing body. Any agency and authority women enjoy emerge from the womb.

Whereas wombs nurture life, pregnancy signifies a range of complex meanings—it has negative and positive valances. Women have learned to negotiate these diverse concepts and associations with their bodies from anatomical definitions to cultural ideals. But the experience of navigating life as a wombed person is stubbornly unchanged.[3] Pregnancy proves a perpetual paradox for female identity. In ways both subtle and obvious, pregnancy has been transformed by modern technology and culture as well as legal, medical, and political reform. Still, women find themselves constrained by their reproductive marking and lack the encouragement and imagination to resignify their embodied situations. The womb underlies this troubling reality.

Woman as womb is not a fixed idea. She can be figured through four archetypes of the wombed body: *Mary*, womb as sacred space; *Athena*, womb as political space; *Venus*, womb as erotic space; and *Barbie*, womb as material space. Archetypal pregnant subjects authorize repressive imaginings about women's bodies, but they also invite powerful resistance. They capture both the negative contours of females who suffer oppression vis-à-vis pregnancy and the positive contours of females who recast pregnancy as an empowering experience. *Athena to Barbie* challenges women's subordination by uncovering models of wombed labor that sanction diverse modes of womanhood. Feminist interrogations of the body can unravel the logic of female identity and label the ideologies that inform them.

Within this exploration of womanhood and wombs, "woman" represents a narrative construction or sign of the female subject rather than an anatomically defined person. Constructing woman as a discursive and iconographic sign helps readers see how archetypes like Athena continue to influence contemporary female identity. Narrative constructions of woman also recognize persons who identify as women but lack uteruses (due to a hysterectomy, for example) as full female subjects. Normatively feminine bodies appear in the ideologies of woman examined here. But such bodies are not identified as essential to the definition of "woman."

Regret pervades this work. For most of philosophy's history, almost no thought has been given to the idea that female embodiment has philosophical significance. The historic equating of the dictum "Know thyself" with "Know thy mind" coupled with the unstated assumption that minds are male have deprived philosophers of grappling with what it means to live in a body, see embodiment as a component of self-identity, and treat bodily signification as a complex element of the human condition. This book is committed to overcoming this loss by honoring embodiment—female embodiment in particular—as worthy of profound philosophical reflection. Along with regret, this work is born of hope that philosophy can recover a practice of valuing women and wombs fully.

For what, *and for whom*, women's bodies may be used remains contested. Exposing the weight of the womb for female experience and identity—*critiquing the womb through the perspective of feminist philosophy*—both challenges the subordination of reproductive bodies and invites a subject-centered reimagining of pregnancy. The pregnant body uniquely elucidates women's struggle for subjectivity: for autonomy, voice, meaning, and standing. Sexually differentiated roles and responsibilities such as childbearing have been invoked to exploit, marginalize, and disempower women. Nuanced readings of the body along with a greater valuing of bodily acts—appreciation for occupations that rely on physical labor and respect for laboring with the body—can also recast the ideology of reproduction in an affirming light. Pregnancy, realized in literal and figurative ways, can offer a woman demonstrative control over her life, allowing her to do what she wishes in an embodied way, not by denying her womb, but by navigating the ambiguity of her embodied identity. *Athena to Barbie* offers a path toward claiming female subjectivity in the face of the significant forces that undermine it.

The archetypal female figure Mary opens this analysis for two reasons. First, the book takes inspiration from Woolf's extended essay *A Room of One's Own*, which begins with Mary. Woolf invokes the Scottish ballad of Mary Hamilton (Hamilton is to be hanged) to exemplify the insignificance of women. She disclaims the "I," the presumed omniscient narrator, in favor of the Marys named in the ballad: Queen Mary, Mary Seaton, Mary Beaton, Mary Carmichael, "and me [Mary Hamilton]."[4] Some readers regard Hamilton as the underlying voice of *A Room of One's Own*, a voice without value as her name "is not a matter of any importance."[5] Although Woolf's stated purpose is to discuss women and fiction, her larger textual aim is to address the insidious problem of female inequality. Woolf asks whether women's progress is possible given their educational, cultural, and economic poverty. Woolf's Marys proffer an answer: women need money and freedom, *a room of their own*, to become fully who they are. The freedom to earn a wage, the courage to pursue one's passions, requires effort and determination. Woolf employs the metaphor of childbirth to describe the outcome of this emancipatory work: "she will put on the body which she has so often laid down," and "she will be born."[6] Her freedom, her self-realization, comes with an ironic cost. "The economists are telling us," Woolf writes, "that Mrs. Seton [*sic*] has had too many children. You must, of course, go on bearing children, but, so they say, in twos and threes, not in tens and twelves."[7] Woolf recognizes that to be born or not to be born—to choose the difficult task of becoming a fully agential self—is a feminist question.[8]

A second reason the book begins with Mary is that the biblical Mary, mother of the Christian Messiah Jesus, is the exemplar of womanhood par excellence. The discourse surrounding pregnancy and motherhood reverberates with Mary's presence. Her performance of pregnancy so thoroughly dominates the ideology of femininity that nearly every claim about the pregnant subject can be traced to her. Reading wombed bodies, then, necessarily begins with Mary and moves thematically through divergent archetypes of pregnant subjects. Mary plays an essential role in the production of female identity and experience.

Mary—and Athena, Venus, and Barbie—materializes the relationship between women's wombs and female subordination. Women remain subordinate to men by multiple measures including access to economic and political power. Women's wombs have everything to do with this social calculation. What the female body is, what it does or performs, and what it represents remain significant for women and the world they inhabit. If a woman is *not* a womb yet *has* a womb, to employ the language of Simone de Beauvoir's *The Second Sex*, she must navigate the changing forces that operate on her body and define her. If a woman is *not a womb* but *has* an *impregnated* womb, she must navigate the sometimes-tacit norms of both womanhood and pregnancy: she is not her womb, but her womb is visible. Her uterus, normally unseen, is on display; physicians measure it, and technicians peer inside it. She cannot dictate its size, nor can she hide it. Her body redefines her, diminishing other aspects of her being and self-identity—her rational capacity, for one thing, and her existential situation, for another. Her womb becomes the element of her embodiment most salient to viewers and, in some cases, to herself, reinforcing an already contracted understanding of the body. In short, the central law of patriarchy—*women must respect the boundaries of their gender*—is heightened during pregnancy (but always present because of woman's reproductive body). The ambiguity of pregnancy offers women an occasion to rethink what it means and how it feels to live, think, and act as a woman.

Feminism cannot resolve the ambiguity of female identity. Being a woman with a womb remains as vexed as ever. But feminist critiques can elevate women's embodied subjectivity by resisting readings of the womb that sanction female subordination. Women should experience their bodies as part of their wholeness and agency in the world. Women must recognize and compel others to recognize embodiment in all its forms as a source and site of human subjectivity. If this analysis of womanhood and wombs succeeds, it will disrupt for a moment, at least among readers, the mediation and regulation of female subjects by calling out oppressive ideologies and norms that operate on wombed bodies. Let us interrogate pregnancy for ways to locate and generate bodily meaning as we search for self.

1

Delivering Mary

Womb as Sacred Space

> Hail Mary, full of grace. Our Lord is with
> you. Blessed are you among women and
> blessed is the fruit of your womb, Jesus.
>
> —The Hail Mary

Mary is remembered and revered for her womb.[1] Her powerful performance of pregnancy looms large in theological imaginings. Yet she transcends theological readings to take on a central archetypal role of the feminine in the Western world. She signs woman *as* womb, a source of sanctifying activity. She places the female body in a spiritual field of meaning, defying reductive readings of wombs and the women who carry them. She makes wombs sacred: wombs perform a divine act. They (re)produce and birth children of God, uniting divinity and humanity. Yet even within this Marian archetype, embodied feminine performances create a normative equivalency between womanhood and motherhood, one that women are right to resist. A woman is not *just* a womb. Nor is she fundamentally an object, an opening, an Other, though she has become these things.[2] Mary's body teems with cultural meanings that enable and disable forms of female agency that women need to live fruitfully.[3] Attending to Mary's womb opens up a fertile space for feminist reflection on the reproductive body, a space that may deliver Mary from a narrow reading of female subjectivity. Reading Mary's womb through a feminist lens serves to reconceive femininity without its embedded, motherly ideals and reimagine the womb as a generative space that produces female practices (and recodes femininity) in literal and metaphoric ways.[4]

Mary is an important archetype of woman because she so thoroughly embodies the paradoxical poles of wombed subjectivity: bodily immanence and miraculous transcendence. She *is and is not* her womb. She *is and is not* a conventional woman. She *can and cannot* control her lived experience. Mary reflects the reality of female personhood: women *are and are not* their pregnant bodies. Women no longer need to argue they are more than a womb. But in what sense *more* is yet to be realized. Conventional views of the feminine—the idea of a distinguishing quality, nature, or essence of woman or a defining, distinctive feature of female experience—retreat from dated scientific tropes. Although woman is not *biologically* "The Sex" any longer, contemporary performances of femininity retain an essentialist edge: woman is a material and semiotic body that reproduces male power. She is already and always defined by cultural readings of her anatomy, by the significations of her bodily parts and the cultural uses and disciplining of her anatomy—for aesthetic pleasure, sexual gratification, and domestic labor, most especially human reproduction. She has yet to fully realize herself as more than a subjugated category of persons: a female person (woman) differentiated from a male person (man) by bodily function (pregnancy) and presentation (femininity). She has yet to fully experience personhood as a subject rather than an object: as an autonomous, rational, moral, and spiritual agent who can deliver herself from subjugation by resignifying what and who she is apart from her reproductive capacity and feminine identity. She has yet to fully activate her womb, a site of literal *and* figurative creative activity, as a source of self-identity.[5]

Pregnancy exposes a submerged and powerful truth about female body-subjects: women's bodies perform personhood in ways that men's bodies do not.[6] Bodies with wombs are circumscribed by their wombed activity (and inactivity). Identifying woman with womb and signifying womb as a sacred and fundamental source of female agency produce an enigmatic tension within pregnant subjectivity—a dual attribution of pregnancy as a passive, generically female, bodily phenomenon and a powerful, feminine, individuating, spiritual activity.

Reading Mary's performance of pregnancy as a sacred, sacrificial act both reinforces and challenges the cultural conception of woman as womb. The signification of womb as sacred authorizes repressions of female sexuality and restrictions on women's reproductive choice. The evangelical Protestant and Roman Catholic espousal of chastity, opposition to abortion, repression of female authority, and conflation of pregnancy with motherhood codify marriage as an essential pathway for female flourishing and a necessary marker of femininity. Marriage's sanctity—the ordination of marriage by God—preserves the womb's divinity.[7] Alternatively, coding womb as sacred thwarts readings of woman as a passive, generic vessel for male occupation and domination. Rereading Mary as a spiritual mother whose womb supports a refusal of oppression recasts pregnancy as an agential phenomenon—as a nonobjectifying element of womanhood and a meaningful component of women's personal identity.[8]

The womb's warrant of female agency resignifies the female body (normatively treated as threatening, sinful, and inferior) as stable, good, and powerful. Active wombs enable women to challenge extant power structures by establishing an authentic ground for opposition to female oppression (pregnancy and motherhood decrease the perceived threat to male power). Active wombs authorize women to speak authoritatively about experiences of injustice despite normative compliance.[9] Motherhood thus permits, rather than forbids, feminist activism. Mary's model of woman as mother and activist motivates a reimagination of pregnant subjectivity: wombed persons as self-directing subjects of their corporeal and spiritual activities.

Feminist inquiries into female subjectivity must grapple with Mary's performance of pregnancy. By shying away from theological imaginings of the womb, we overlook the powerful force Mary exerts on the lives of women, mothers and nonmothers alike. Mary exposes important ontological and psychological tensions that inform our understanding of womanhood and shape the cultural status of women: woman as feminine object (a passive, generic, bodily vessel) versus woman as subversive agent (an active—and activist—mother figure). Her dual prescriptive and transgressive performance of womanhood complicates female subjectivity. But it also provides good reason to reconceive pregnancy's role in grounding women's agency and forging personal identity. Feminists will betray not just Mary but all women if they refuse her model of woman and signification of womb out of hand. Forsaking Mary undermines the very subjectivity she authorizes by ruling out agential forms of motherhood and spiritual significations of feminine labor.[10]

Mary as Passive Vessel

Mary, or Miriam, the Jewish mother of Jesus of Nazareth, is mentioned infrequently in the New Testament. We know almost nothing about her personal history.[11] She is a necessary but ancillary figure in biblical Scripture and Christian theology.[12] The Gospel of Matthew describes her as an unexpectant but willing young mother whose maternity threatens the political order of the day: she is the *Theotokos* (God-bearer), the woman who dares to undermine royal power by birthing the ruler of a counter-kingdom.[13] The Gospel of Luke expands her roles beyond mother to include those of disciple and prophet.[14] John's Gospel and the book of Acts elevate her standing among Jesus's followers, foreshadowing her motherhood of the church.[15] Mary becomes the New Eve (or Second Eve), the woman who accepts God by implanting the fruit of the Holy Spirit in her womb. Eve, by contrast, rejects God; she eats the fruit.[16]

Despite the sparse biblical information about her historic reception, Mary is highly conspicuous within the Abrahamic traditions.[17] She is recognized by Jews as a fellow sufferer, venerated by Roman Catholics for her intimacy with God, and honored by Protestants for her redemptive character.[18] The Qur'an dedicates an entire sura to Mary (Maryam), the only chapter devoted to a woman. Late medieval descriptions of her reflect a myriad of Marian names, images, and associations: "mirror of justice," "house of gold," and "gate of heaven" among them.[19] Modern books, buildings, art objects, and countless other artifacts pay homage to her life.[20] Mary is a venerated and complex figure—saint, prophet, teacher, servant, humble Jewish woman. She is a global and eternal figure, all because of her womb.[21]

Mary codifies the idea of woman as vessel, a literal and figurative container for the creation and sustenance of others. Moreover, her container is pure: she is a virgin at least through conception.[22] These intertwined Marian concepts—*woman as womb* and *woman as pure*—produce uncompromising performances of womanhood.[23] Contemporary purity movements in conservative Roman Catholic and evangelical Protestant circles appropriate Mary's purity as a lifestyle guide. Purity advocates not only read Mary along a binary—woman is either pure and passive or worldly and agential—they ascribe the restrictive attributes (purity and passivity) to her character, which constrain her subjectivity and prohibit a more diverse and complex embodiment. Purity advocates also conflate purity and passivity with chastity and proclaim chasteness a cardinal Christian virtue. Mary's virginity is, therefore, read in literal terms. Hence one must be celibate to mirror Mary.[24]

"Purity rings" and "sexual sobriety chips" outwardly signify and honor girls (and boys, though they are peripheral to the movement) who commit themselves to sexual abstinence.[25] Virginity, understood as biological, is aspirational, since God favored it in the example of Mary. Because Mary is a female exemplar, virginity is taken to be a uniquely feminine marker of virtue; that is, to be a "good girl" is to be chaste. Women who explore sexuality outside of the proper bounds of marriage are degraded: they are "slutty," "easy," "fast," and "loose." Beyond that, they are regarded as the source of male sin, like Eve before them, who is seen as the first and worst sinner.[26] Right-leaning prescriptions of womanhood help explain conservative attitudes toward female embodiment.[27] Beyond the social judgment and alienation one or one's family may experience because of violative sexual behavior, conservatives regard sexual impropriety as a major stumbling block for salvation.[28] So sexuality is carefully circumscribed: intercourse is permissible in the confines of heterosexual marriage for the primary purpose of procreation and emotional connection.[29]

For conservative Roman Catholics and Protestants, Scripture supports opposition to abortion by signifying the womb as divine:

> *For it was you who formed my inward parts;*
> *   you knit me together in my mother's womb.*
> *I praise you for I am fearfully and wonderfully made.*
> *   Wonderful are your works;*
> *   that I know very well.*

Psalm 139:13–14

The psalmist's underlying claim is that a woman's womb is not her own. She cannot declare meaningful ownership over her reproductive processes nor integrate them into her self-identity because God is the activator and agent of her wombed activity. The child narrator of the Psalm—who identifies God, the child's spiritual father, as the source of his or her existence—further reinforces woman's alienation from her embodied experiences and effectively undermines her role in the creation of life. The mother is represented as a passive medium for God's creative work; her womb is a sacred space situated inertly in her body and disassociated from her rational activities. She is thus a voiceless and powerless character with no authoritative (or legitimate, per pro-life politics) claim to her body or her womb—or, perhaps, even the child formed within them.[30] Her projected essence (womb) and identity (mother) evaporate as the psalmist's erasure of woman becomes complete. In this scheme, male agency is conditioned on female submission.

An additional challenge of Psalm 139 is the refusal of a phenomenology of pregnancy. Women who have birthed children know that the transition from "pregnant woman" to "mother" is fluid. Motherhood represents an embodied shift in self-conception and self-identity that unfolds over time, including, for some women, after the birth of their babies.[31] The psalmist flattens the experience of motherhood into a single moment, equating conception and motherhood temporally and logically.

Whereas good Christian girls are chaste, good Christian women are devoted mothers. Mary serves again as a powerful role model for a Christian archetype of feminine identity. Mary's performance of motherhood aligns with the Psalms: it *begins with* maternity.[32] Her identity as a mother extends beyond the singular conception, birth, and death of her son, Jesus, to the conception and birthing of the church itself. She sustains a protracted maternity through her desire to "mother" everything her son wills.[33] Mary, the mother of Jesus, operates as the figurative mother of the church.[34]

Mary's pregnancy is typically read as a cooperative exercise with God, a foregrounding of free will in the history of salvation.[35] She consents to, and celebrates in song,

God's merciful work.[36] But troubling elements of obedience appear to ensure Mary's maternity. A young Jewish virgin suspends her will to submit to God's will—"Behold, I am the handmaid of the Lord. May it be done to me according to your word"—to enable the salvation of the human race as prophesied in the Jewish faith.[37] The primary (active) work is the Spirit's work (Luke 1:35–37). Mary's submission and obedience, her secondary (passive) work, operationalizes her individual performance of motherhood and serves to justify the disciplining of women's wills and bodies collectively: women must obey, submit, and keep silent. Chaste while single, women must be fruitful once married.

Conventional readings of Christian doctrine prescribe women's obedience to men in the context of the church and home ("a wife is to submit herself graciously to the servant leadership of her husband . . .").[38] Early Christian theologians even condition the Eve-Mary parallel on obedience: Eve's disobedience destroys the human race, whereas Mary's obedience saves it.[39] Eve's rejection of the Holy Spirit (she eats the forbidden fruit) and Mary's acceptance of the Holy Spirit (she allows the fruit to be implanted in her womb) produce comparable, embodied acts. Eve's and Mary's respective choices, despite their opposing significations, produce shared, embodied consequences: Eve and Mary will bear children and suffer in childbirth, a dual reinforcement of women's bodily nature. Women's power is rooted in maternity, a sign of female subordination. Obedience produces docile, maternal bodies that operate as ideal feminine subjects.[40]

A conservative codification of womanhood denies women the experience and signification of their bodies as dominant. The normalization of female bodies as subordinate also subverts liberal explorations of female identity that see women as individuated subjects (individuals). The church's appeal to female obedience also recalls high incidences of sexual, emotional, and physical abuse by family members and clergy.[41] Because the Marian archetype of womanhood is tacitly conditioned on obedience (and its associative qualities of docility and submissiveness), the implications for women go beyond religious and marital relationships. Once obedience is accepted as an underlying justification for maternity—a justification for the performance of *woman as womb*—women who elect not to have children or are infertile are suspect in a Marian-Christian scheme. They are not fruitful, in defiance of the Biblical mandate; they do not multiply in the literal sense of God's law. Moreover, their lack of fruitfulness flouts the maxim for God's blessing outlined in The Hail Mary, a prayer of the Rosary, that opens this chapter: motherhood is the ultimate fulfillment of womanhood. God blesses Mary because she is a female exemplar: her womb bears fruit, a child, who is also blessed. Women who defy Abrahamic constructions of femininity are both deviant and, it follows from the prayer, cursed. Deviance is subsequently used as a justification for marginalizing and shaming women without children: they have violated feminine norms ordained by God. God's subsequent curse amounts to a final rejection of their nonmaternal performance of woman. These nasty women broke God's law.[42]

Chastity in singleness and fruitfulness in marriage engender prescriptive codes of womanhood and enforce the normative view that *woman is but a womb*. The Abrahamic ideal restricts a woman's embodied agency and identity to motherhood: "Yet she will be saved through childbearing, provided they continue in faith and love and holiness, with modesty" (1 Timothy 2:15). Fortunately, other readings, including feminist readings, of women's nature and identity can deliver Mary from an inherently subordinate and maternal position. Woman as womb is not the only reading the Abrahamic tradition invites.

Mary as Agential Womb

The religious emphasis on Mary as mother has roots in a Christ-centered or christotypical Mariology.[43] Such a Mariology describes Mary's value and privilege as arising from her association with her son, Jesus, and not from any independent affiliation with the divine or other prophetic practices. Her power, somewhat like the power of influential Protestant pastors' wives, is rooted in male power. Although the Roman Catholic Church has affirmed other modes of reading Mary and other forms of Marian theology—see Paul VI's 1974 apostolic exhortation *Marialis Cultus*, for example, which characterizes Mary as "a woman who did not hesitate to proclaim that God vindicates the humble and the oppressed, and removes the powerful people of this world from their privileged positions"[44]—the papacy continues to speak the language of christotypical Mariology.[45]

Saint John Paul II, Benedict XVI, and Francis have invoked christotypical language to bolster the global devotional piety that regards Mary as the active dispenser of mercy.[46]

Mary's virtuous embodiment, her infinite goodness and power, is believed to justify the Catholic devotional practice of intercessory prayers: Mary can, thanks to her purity and moral perfection, assist with every human need.[47] The belief in her power to intercede is based on the mother's close connection to her son.[48] Indeed, her acquisition of goodness is predicated on her womb. The intimate binding of her flesh with that of Christ—"Christ's flesh is the flesh of her flesh (as Eve's was of Adam)"—generates a unity with God so that her own flesh is also God's flesh.[49] Her rational assent to the Holy Spirit is thus secondary to her physical assent.[50]

While the bodily dimensions of christotypical readings have some value for feminist philosophy—they nicely challenge the body's assigned negative value and reassess its role in perpetuating women's inferior status—the diminishment of Mary's rational assent reinforces the idea of pregnancy as a physical phenomenon alone. Her reproductive body becomes a docile, inert thing.[51] Stripped of subjectivity, agency, and rationality, Mary loses the capacity to fully engage the phenomenological richness and liberating potential of pregnancy. Christotypical readings thus reinscribe the paradoxical logic of woman's power as mother, a power rooted in submission. Repressing Mary's subjectivity reinforces male power and dominance.

If, on the other hand, Mary subverts male power by sharing volition with God—if she chooses to enter into relationship with the divine—the tradition of piety surrounding devotion to merciful (and maternal) Mary takes a radical turn. By choosing maternity, Mary's assent becomes a personal act that authorizes a unique and agential mothering of child and church.[52] By freeing pregnancy from a power relation that subordinates the feminine to the masculine, Mary liberates pregnancy from its circumscribed passivity. Like Jesus who reverses the Edenic curse and frees humans from social oppression, Mary reverses the material and maternal dimensions of this curse and frees women from embodied objectivity. Pregnancy becomes *a chosen activity* in both literal and figurative senses. Moreover, figurative pregnancies—women's birthing of ideas, systems, and institutions—ameliorate the masculine marking of intellectual and spiritual activities that enforce female subordination.[53] The womb thus operates both as a sacred space itself *and* as a creator of sacred spaces, making female subjectivity both reproductive *and* productive. Wombs can deliver women.

A powerful idea of Mary as spiritual mother dominates religious iconography from the third to fifteenth centuries CE. *Maria lactans* (the nursing Madonna) imagery presents the Virgin breastfeeding the infant Jesus. The nurturing mother, "the wet-nurse of salvation," is a female symbol of God's love.[54] Holiness surrounds and radiates from Mary in this example titled *The Nursing Madonna*. Her common clothing represents the accessibility of salvation to every hungry sinner, a subversion of the state's arbitrary and hierarchical judgment.[55] The cradling of Mary's body in a walnut seed, a traditional fertility symbol, reflects her spiritual fruitfulness.[56] She inspires wisdom and spiritual practices in others. In Christian culture, the walnut seed has also come to symbolize the Trinity. Mary's placement illustrates her proximity to God, a further indication of her spiritual authority and autonomy.[57]

Anonymous Master of Bruges, *Nursing Madonna* (*Madonna Lactans*), 16th century, Museu de Aveiro, Portugal.

Because it was reasonable for viewers to believe that Mary would have nursed her infant child, it was natural to embrace the Virgin as the nourishing mother of the church. The construction of femininity that warrants Mary's identity as a spiritual mother is properly embodied and powerfully agential. She bares her breast as a gesture of female supplication to Christ when asking for mercy for sinners.[58] Her milk parallels the role of the blood of Christ in Christian worship: a source of unity in salvation.[59] "By the Middle Ages, 'lactation miracles' and 'milk shrines' sprang up across the Christian world" in Eastern Orthodox and Catholic communities.[60] The breast's lactating function is regarded as natural and good rather than abject; it serves as a source of female power.

The commanding image of Mary as spiritual mother changes in the sixteenth century when clerical writers, following the Council of Trent, oppose nudity in religious subjects. *Maria lactans* iconography also fades from view after the advent of movable type and the printing press. Early forms of pornography sexualize women's bodies in the popular imagination while the printing press facilitates the circulation of anatomical drawings for medical study. These examples of mass communication demystify the body and challenge biblical views of the body as a reflection of God.[61]

The mass production of the Bible also contributes to the disappearance of *Maria lactans*.[62] The printing of Scripture in the vernacular coupled with Protestantism's focus on text over imagery undermine the efficacy of Mary's breast as a sign of holy providence.[63] Once the breast is codified as an object of medical study and inscribed with sexual desire, it disappears as a subject of sacred desire entirely.[64]

Mary's lactating breasts, once a symbol of her salvific power and closeness with God, are supplanted by her son's crucified body—the suffering Jesus on the cross—as "the dominant motif of Christianity."[65] The suppression of the feminine is especially troubling in cultural contexts that are hostile to women and serve to objectify, sexualize, and degrade them. Imagining the Virgin mother as inertly maternal refuses Mary the properly sororal (sisterly) and prophetic (knowing) identity her active womb warrants.[66] Pregnancy, childbirth, and other (bodily) female activities connect and educate women. The womb operates as a distinctive source of knowledge and care: women connect, empathize, and teach one another through the joy, pain, and sorrow of pregnancy, childbirth, and motherhood. Stripping away Mary's (women's) epistemic and emotional activities flattens her cognitive, subjective engagement with the world: Mary becomes an inert object. Delivering Mary from this performance of pregnancy requires a reimagination of the womb as a generative space for female agency in ways both literal and metaphorical.[67]

Mary as Woman

Marian constructions make it difficult to imagine Mary in her everyday life in Nazareth, a poor province of the Roman Empire. She presumably performs the customary duties of women in ancient farming communities. She carts well water, shops at the marketplace, and prepares meals for her family. She weaves cloth and makes clothing appropriate for different seasons. She cares for her husband, Joseph, a busy carpenter, as well as elderly family members and friends. She attends religious services and feasts. She socializes with Galilean women, enjoying news from around the Mediterranean world. She maintains herself, staying fit and clean, regularly washing and oiling her long, braided hair. She assists with crop and animal production. She disciplines her children, including her precocious first child, Jesus.[68]

Normative constraints on the feminine prohibit Mary from disciplining her children. The passive subjectivity she is ascribed—*woman as womb* and *womb as sacred space*—renders female acts of discipline subversive. In the painting *Young Virgin Spanking the Infant Jesus in Front of Three Witnesses*, the twentieth-century German artist Max Ernst portrays Mary striking Jesus on his naked body while onlookers (friends) observe her with skepticism and disdain. Ernst's anthropological approach defies modern constructions of female identity by reinscribing the feminine with maternal and spiritual authority (Mary wears a halo). The elongated Christ child crosses his ankles and extends his arms as if in a crucifixion scene, anticipating his death on the cross, a final punishment. His bottom bears the mark of Mary's anger. She is swift and defiant. Ernst references and overturns the work of Parmigianino, the sixteenth-century Italian mannerist who indulges iconographic renderings of a sensuous, beatified, adored and adoring mother. Mary bears the traditional blue that appears on the legs of

Parmigianino's *Madonna with the Long Neck*, but she also dons a customary red dress to indicate how ordinary she (and her act of discipline) is.[69] Ernst thus normalizes Marian authority.

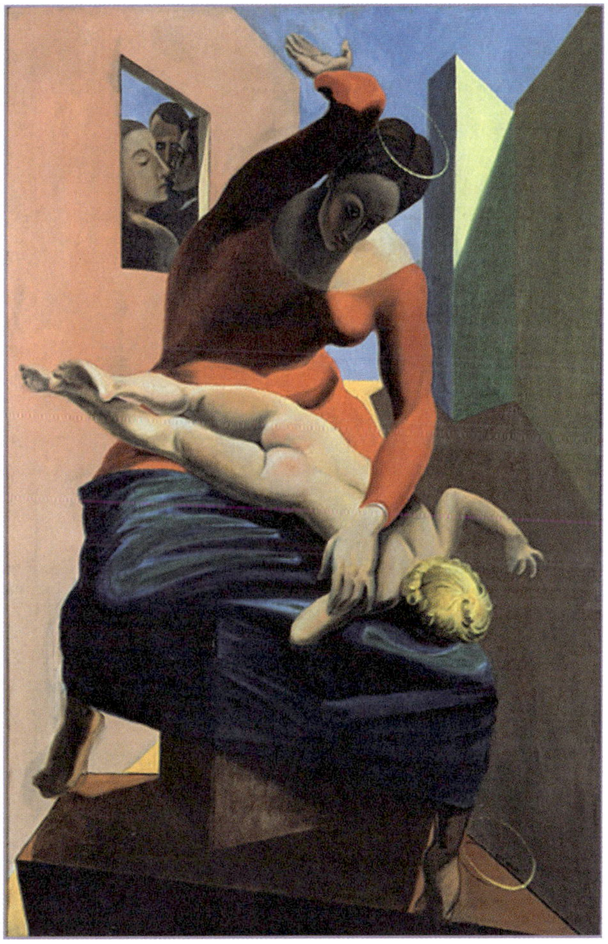

Max Ernst, *The Virgin Chastising the Christ Child before Three Witnesses: André Breton, Paul Éluard and the Painter*, 1926, Museum Ludwig, Cologne, Germany, Photo by: Rheinisches Bildarchiv Köln.

Christotypical Mariology emphasizes Mary's passiveness, her submission to authority, her acceptance of female subordination, and her expressions of femininity that suppress female authority. Ernst shows that Mary's performance of womanhood does not have to erase her personhood. Mary's cooperation with God and subsequent mothering of the church sanction the disciplinary activities that Ernst depicts. Some Jewish and early Greco-Roman sources suggest that Mary's life may have been less restrictive than scholars have assumed.[70] If we resist reading Mary as an agential woman, we also refuse women a powerful model of female subjectivity and authority.[71]

Feminist Engagement with the Sacred Womb

Mary continues to exert a powerful influence on the readings and reimaginations of pregnant bodies today. The pop icon Beyoncé (Queen B) issues a provocative reimagining of Mary in this photograph of herself as the apparition of the blessed Virgin of Guadalupe.[72] Our Lady of Guadalupe appeared as an apparition before Saint Juan Diego, a Christian convert, in 1531. Today she serves a dual religious and political function: she is a source of Roman Catholic devotion and a national symbol of Mexico.

Like Our Lady, Queen B is a female cultural icon. Her artistic genius inspires her fans' veneration of her as an exemplar of feminine strength. Beyoncé appropriates the symbolic accoutrement of the Virgin Mary to reinscribe the culturally laden figure of the Virgin Mother. Her halo of flowers grants

Juan de Sáenz, *Virgen de Guadalupe con las cuatro apariciones* by Juan de Sáenz, c.1777, Museo Soumaya, Mexico City, Mexico.

Beyoncé; Instagram

divinity to nature rather than God, a semiotic privileging of
the feminine over the masculine order and a reclamation
of woman's divine power. Her hands hug her swollen, pregnant abdomen to signal the womb as a profound source of
female power over and against the power of the heavenly
Father whom the blessed Virgin petitions in her clasped-
handed prayer. To reinforce her feminine power, Beyoncé
assumes the yogic pose of *Virasana* or the hero's pose, symbolizing her reputation as a forceful female figure. Beyoncé
is the new Eve, the new Mary, the Black queen mother.[73]
She is a heroic and *delivered* woman.

Today, the idea of womb as sacred is tied to politically
right-of-center policies regarding reproductive choice, such
as the newly resurrected "heartbeat bills" in Alabama, Geor-
gia, Mississippi, Missouri, Kentucky, Texas, and elsewhere.
The bills propose to deny pregnant women access to lawful
abortions after the medical detection of a fetal heartbeat
(the Texas bill was recently signed into law). Their implicit
logic is that since the womb is a sacred space (carrying life),
it does not belong to any one person, even if that person is
the mother.[74] The cultural inclination to call infants and
unborn children "angels" or "miracles" also reinforces the
implicit belief that the womb is divine; that is, if babies
are angels, they belong ultimately to God rather than their
parents or themselves. If babies are miracles, God ordained
their creation. Pregnant women's use of *#blessed* on social
media reflects a popular spiritual orientation toward pregnancy: pregnancy is a singularly spiritual activity decreed
by God.[75] Even the modern fascination with the ultrasound

can be interpreted as a sacred ritual (father and mother are worshippers, the infant is the holy one, and the doctor is the priest). Blurry sonogram images evoke and are often treated as religious icons.[76]

Women who live in Mary's shadow feel pressure to serve as vessels for others' lives, literally and figuratively. The presumed sacredness of pregnancy attached to Mary— mother of God, queen of heaven, saint of motherhood, exemplar of fertility—produces restrictive as well as liberating paths for understanding and experiencing embodied subjectivity: pregnancy as a dual embodiment of female subordination and empowerment. Reproductive restrictions aside, the idea that pregnancy transcends familial and social realms and enjoys spiritual significance may facilitate women's experiences of their pregnant bodies as empowering rather than threatening.[77] Mary as spiritual mother exhibits the power to deliver the oppressed from oppression.[78] This reimagined, expansive performance of feminine subjectivity gives Mary highly agential identities: sister, prophet, activist. Feminists need a Mary who apprehends herself as a woman and an individual whose womb constitutes some, though not all, of her sense of self.

Overly spiritual renderings of Mary may also prevent women from experiencing their wombs (and bodies) as their own. Modern Mariology has circumscribed women's spiritual, social, and economic authority by portraying female power as submission. Recapitulations of male power and spiritual authority produce passive bodies that code femininity as an inert, passive, female performance. Purity, regarded as an essential feminine feature, is materialized on the body as virginity. Venerating Mary and celebrating women whose flourishing is inextricably tied to male flourishing can undermine women's power and agency, especially in the sociopolitical context of women's inequality and female misogyny. It remains unclear whether the visibility of female pregnancy elevates or diminishes women's status. Mary's story of divine conception dramatizes the still uncanny nature of pregnancy. She sets the stage for Athena's archetypal performance of pregnancy as a political activity: a reinscription of the female role with decidedly male duties. Athena—*woman*, *goddess*, *warrior*, and *craftsman*—signifies womb as political space.

2

Conquering Athena

Womb as Political Space

> Brave, unconcerned, mocking, violent—thus
> wisdom wants us: she is a woman and
> always loves only a warrior.
> —Friedrich Nietzsche

Athena, the "woman-goddess" of Greek mythology, presents an audacious portrait of pregnancy.[1] She is, like Mary, a virgin. Her virginity is intimately tied to her unique embodiment: she is neither birthed by a woman nor gives birth herself.[2] The warrior-goddess emerges out of the head of Zeus fully formed and armed for battle. She personifies wisdom and war. She is, like elite men of antiquity, civilized, urban, and politically engaged. She preserves her feminine identity through the patronage of crafts like needlework and weaving.[3] Her affiliation with warfare casts her as masculine and allows her entry into a public, male space. She thus assigns to the female role decidedly male duties. She also redefines motherhood, extending the protection of one's children to the protection of all Athenians, a militaristic responsibility. *Conquering* Athena defeats (conquers) and succumbs to (is conquered by) male power, representing the negative and positive valences of female subjectivity. Athena—*woman*, *goddess*, *warrior*, and *craftsman*—signifies womb as political space.

Athena's appearance in the polis is aptly read as either a female intrusion into the male sphere or a remarkable expansion of the feminine reproductive role.[4] She expresses intelligence, an attribute reserved for men in the ancient world. She embodies political authority and establishes a civic order, a radically male move. She challenges traditional female ties to the home, resisting woman's early identification with domestic labor.[5] Her exploitation of gender ambiguity effectively makes space for female participation in the public arena and rebrands reproductivity as a rational act.[6] Yet the political and epistemic advancements Athena models come with a dramatic twist: *she is celibate.*

Athena "mates neither with gods nor with mortals."[7] She represses her sexual desire for the sake of civic ideals.[8] She reasons and strategizes, eschewing the bodily dimensions of female life. She enacts a political performance of pregnancy—and models mother as civic leader—by birthing and securing the vitality of the city.[9] She thus instantiates the exclusion of the feminine from a masculine world: *women birth bodies*, a feminine task, or *women birth ideas*, a masculine task.[10] The symbolic orders of femininity and masculinity refuse one another.

Athena's archetype of pregnancy, a progressive model of political productivity that anticipates modern feminist goals, is conditioned on the suppression of the feminine body. She erupts from a male mind, encoded to perform pregnancy as a political practice: Athena births civic ideas, institutions, and public goods.[11] Her subjugation of the womb is therefore a function of her masculine performance of womanhood. Her signification of female labor and birth as *unwombed* activities makes explicit the price of a woman's entry into a man's world: assent to masculine norms and values. Athena (as well as Mary, Venus, and Barbie) dutifully conforms to the male social order by appropriating and displaying masculine ideals.[12]

Woolf's figurative use of birth, a metaphor for female emancipation, applies nicely to Athena's situation, a situation that plays out in the lives of women who covet political influence and professional advancement yet feel pressure (or a desire) to become wives and mothers.[13] Being female in a male world—negotiating the logic and ideology of the feminine order with its antecedent roles and identities—is a complex task. The wise, conquering, woman-goddess Athena puts on the body that enables her civic leadership, a body that *reads* male.[14]

Athena as Immaterial Womb

Apollodorus (Pseudo-Apollodorus) recounts the story of Athena's birth in *The Library* or *Bibliotheca*, a second-century BCE text depicted here in a black-figure bowl by the potter Phrynos in 540 BCE: "And when the time came for the birth to take place, Prometheus, or as others say, Hephaestus, struck the head of Zeus with an ax."[15] The ax, or the mythic headache that precedes its blow, produces Zeus's requisite labor pains in the absence of a female uterus. The myth also reports that Zeus has swallowed the primordial Metis, his first wife and the Titan goddess of wisdom, having been warned she would threaten his power. Metis was pregnant with Athena, so Zeus's murderous actions deprive Athena of a mother. Metis does not abandon her daughter to male violence, however. Instead, she sets to work inside

The Phrynos Painter, *Birth of Athena*, black-figured lip-cup, c. 555 BCE, British Museum, England.

Zeus's head and crafts Athena a set of protective armor. The clamor of her work produces Zeus's debilitating headache. His pain becomes so unbearable, he welcomes the ax's rupturing force. Athena is born fortified for the male world.[16]

Athena's birth constitutes the birth of a world without women. She represents a society conceived in the male imaginary rather than the female womb. Masculine conceptions of the social order appeal to transcendence as an organizing principle. Athena, for example, materializes as an adult who transcends the developmental processes of human existence; as a political construct, she privileges principles rather than practices of cooperation and relies on ideology for social cohesion. By contrast, feminine conceptions of the social order dwell in immanence—in human interchanges organized around birth, life, and death—and appeal to human needs, like food and sex, and social practices to bridge political divides. When Zeus appropriates the birthing process for himself, he displaces women from the Greek civic and cultural imagination, a symbolic and violent repression of the feminine order.[17] The attempted erasure of women from civic life sets the stage for pernicious female oppression in every subsequent century.

Female inequality extends beyond political disenfranchisement and unequal pay. Misogyny, hostile work environments, and a devaluing of feminine work contribute to women's inferior status. Women are seen as morally and intellectually suspect and lacking agency because of their inferior, bodily (wombed) nature. They are deprived of parity with men in recognized degrees of dignity, integrity, and authority.

Athena dramatizes the womb's role in women's situation by suspending wombed activities and performing masculine duties, duties that secure her personal power and political engagement.

The cultural suppression of the womb—the literal and symbolic diminishment of the female body and its reproductive activities—does not destroy female power entirely. Metis illustrates this truth through her invisible labor inside Zeus's mind: she transforms Athena into a warrior mother who gives birth to politics. But the womb's suppression nonetheless serves to subjugate women to a "natural" state of immanence—housekeeping, cooking, childbearing, and other forms of bodily labor normalized as feminine. The feminine tie to bodily immanence jeopardizes women's political engagement on practical and theoretical levels. The use of the female body for caregiving depletes time and energy for politics and any nondomestic activities. Thwarting femininity to enter the political sphere, if universalized, undermines the production of the masculine social order: women must produce (birth) the men who run the polis. Women who defy normative gender expectations— by refusing caregiving duties or by occupying political roles—code as male in the social world. "Masculine" women gain some personal agency by assuming male functions, but they ultimately subvert women's equality by decoupling the wombed body from female identity. Because female agency is conditioned on wombed activities, as the Mary example shows, detaching female identity from a full range of (re)productive activities, real and metaphoric, dissuades women from integrating bodily activities into their self-identity. Erasing the female body in constructions of human subjectivity also reinforces male bodies as naturally (normatively) agential: men are conceived as self-directing, while women are conceived as other directing.

The masculine coding of women like Athena is reinforced through normative practices that affirm feminine behaviors. Because feminine norms proscribe unfeminine behaviors, masculine women threaten embodied subjectivity on both personal and public fronts—through self-disorder (by detaching femininity from woman's self-identity) and civil disorder (by disrupting male control over public goods). Unfeminine female behaviors imply psychosocial malformation and, therefore, abnormality. Woman's body and mind are therefore incapable of meeting the conditions for personhood. Unfeminine female behaviors also challenge the two-sphere system of human activity. Femininity allocates women to a private, female sphere. Private-sphere activities, like cooking, cleaning, and caregiving, stabilize the feminine order. Women who follow Athena and leave the private sphere for the public sphere threaten the masculine order by disclaiming male power, suggesting male impotence.[18] Athena represents the dual political valences of masculine womanhood. She is a *conquering* female—a female who overcomes male power by resignifying her womb as political space—and a female who succumbs to male power by denying her womb and assuming a masculine performance of woman. Athena's archetype of womanhood has purchase with women because she embodies the multivalent experience of female subjectivity—the trade-offs of having public responsibilities and roles outside of the home and family.

Authentic experiences and expressions of human subjectivity require female access to private and public spheres of activities regardless of how these activities are gendered. But resistance is everywhere. Athena's instantiation of the feared, masculine woman undermines the sexual binary that supports a division of labor and sustains male privilege. Women's performance of domestic duties frees men to focus time and attention on nondomestic activities. Domestic activities garner less economic and social value than nondomestic tasks, mirroring women's and men's unequal value. Gender norms such as male autonomy also safeguard masculine principles of civil organization, leadership, and control. By rejecting (or transcending) gender norms like Athena, we can expose masculine principles for critique and subvert the sexual division that reinforces woman's passive, abject, biological signification and duties.

Beyond the practical and theoretical problems with male hegemony, suppressing femininity enables masculine norms to operate as universal ideals. Feminine ways of being and knowing—practices rooted in reproductive labor and care for others—lose their existential and epistemic value in the face of male privilege. Women's embodied engagement in the world also exerts no real political force because the idealization of masculinity forecloses the construction of social visions that enable immanence and transcendence to coexist and share equal weight. The critical question is not whether female agency allows for women's political engagement but whether women's political engagement can be reconciled with distinctively feminine (bodily) performances of womanhood.

Athena as Unfeminine Womb

Athena's appropriation of masculine norms like physical strength and wisdom enables her to perform motherhood as civic leadership. Her political signification of womb challenges the definitive, biological construction of woman as a reproductive creature in important ways.[19] Her wholesale transformation of female identity requires, of course, divine effort.

Woman's bodily immanence is critical to the development of human civilization.[20] Prehistoric fertility cults and ancient epigraphic, literary, and archaeological records reveal the widespread worship of female pregnancy and reproduction.[21] Over time, the normalized use of women's bodies for birthing children and caring for families, along with the rise of modern labor, marked the womb as a defining element of woman's situation in the world and her "natural, normal" destiny. Today the twin ideologies of femininity and motherhood serve to align and identify women with domestic labor almost exclusively.

The cultural investment in woman as womb makes Athena's example of a disembodied, rational, and political woman leader even more extraordinary. Athena's bold appropriation of the womb for the purpose of birthing ideas functions as an embodied act of male civic engagement and a political performance of pregnancy. She repositions and resignifies the material body as inessential to womanhood, a move that subverts the ideology of woman as child bearer and recasts females as rational rather than bodily creatures. Her symbolic emancipation of women from bodily labor and pain invites broader resistance to female exclusion from the world. She secures for women the most powerful political weapon of the male world: *the mind*.[22]

Priestesses and female cult figures from the Archaic through the Hellenistic periods draw on Athena's masculinity to construct novel forms of agency and identity within a complex system of male power.[23] Textual sources, inscribed dedications, and cultural objects show that ancient Greek women engaged in important religious roles and rituals, acts of transcendence beyond narrow, bodily, and sexual constructions of womanhood that point to Athena's influence.[24] Aristophanes's fifth-century BCE comedy *Lysistrata* depicts the seizure of the Athenian Acropolis by the city's women, a meaningful allusion to the goddess herself. Though these women are deprived of citizenship, they use their sexual (bodily) power over men to force an end to the Peloponnesian War: no peace, no sex.[25]

Athena's archetypal woman, a woman who refuses the biological womb in favor of political authority, symbolizes one of several ways that women have sought to resolve the vexed nature of womanhood as they search for self. Our modern appropriation of Athena should not, however, overshadow her important function in her own time. Ancient exercises of female agency exemplify the importance of Athena's mythic scheme in the Greek civic imagination. For instance, the laws and political processes of ancient Greece deny women political standing.[26] But the mythic ideals embodied by Athena make space for women in ancient civic practices. Women of antiquity not only exercise informal power over monetary decisions and household property, but they also hold *de facto* political offices in cultic activities.[27] Athena legitimates women as real political players in the civic experience and, therefore, serves as a helpful and hopeful archetype of woman.[28]

Athena's archetype of pregnancy as a political activity raises perennial questions about women's relationship to the state. Women have enjoyed less political power and freedom than men despite progressive social movements and philosophies.[29] The democratic revolutions of eighteenth-century Europe and America, buttressed by Enlightenment arguments for equality, were ripe for the materialization of a real-life Athena: *rational, nonsexual,* and *political.* Yet unlike the women of ancient Athens, European and American women have no Athena in their cultural and civic imaginations to which they can appeal for inspiration. They lack a symbol system for female rationality: the male alone is coded as rational (and so the femininity of intellectual female politicians like Margaret Thatcher, Hillary Clinton, and Elizabeth Warren—as well as Golda Meir and Indira Gandhi—is questioned).[30] Like the christotypical readings of Christianity that push Mary to the periphery, eighteenth-century conceptions of rationality are both male-centric and masculine.[31] It is not accidental that Descartes's cogito is embedded in a male body.

Enlightenment significations of reason as male persist in contemporary articulations of rationality. Hannah Arendt valorizes action (male, public sphere) over labor (female, private sphere) in ways that diminish women's embodied labor reminiscent of Beauvoir—even though Arendt, ironically, declines to acknowledge any affinity between Beauvoir's work and her concerns with sources of authoritarianism and oppression.[32] The term *vita activa*, which emerges early as a core idea in the Western tradition of political thought, means "a life devoted to public-political matters."[33] *Vita activa* designates three fundamental human activities: labor, work, and action. Labor is an activity that corresponds to the biological processes of the human body; life is the human condition of labor. Work is an activity that corresponds to the unnaturalness of human existence—work provides an artificial world of things different from natural objects. And action is an activity (the only activity) that goes on directly between men (not Man) without the intermediary of things or matter; men live on the earth and inhabit the world.[34] Deprivation is the tragic outcome of laboring as a woman, according to Arendt: "To live an entirely private life means above all to be deprived of things essential to a truly human life: to be deprived of the reality that comes from being seen and heard by others, to be deprived of an 'objective' relationship with them that comes from being related to and separated from them through the intermediary of a common world of things, to be deprived of the possibility of achieving something more permanent than life itself."[35] The public-private distinction with its added masculine and feminine connotations makes impossible the idea of a laboring, working, and active woman on Arendt's account. Women must, in other words, become like men to enter the public sphere, a claim Athena paradoxically subverts.

We recognize now that because gender is mapped onto a binary, male-female sexed system, appeals to female rationality constitute a destabilizing breach of the male-female binary. Granting woman rationality, a masculine faculty, threatens female identity by subverting feminine constructions of womanhood and challenges male identity by contesting the sexual division of labor. Conquering Athena appropriates mind as womb and births the polis. Although her subversive performance of motherhood authorizes women's engagement with the public sphere, it also signifies a repression of the feminine order.[36] Athena's introduction of woman as thinker and leader into the female imaginary comes with a price. Conquering female (bodily) subjectivity, refusing one's embodied womb, constitutes a masculine act that codes Athena as male. Becoming a woman involves negotiating the gendered boundaries of body and mind.

Athena as Warrior

Athena's embedded presence in the civic and cultural imagination of ancient Greece generates a practical, if not ideological, reconception of life with a womb. She births and protects male citizens while also empowering women to assume a similar responsibility for civic and social order. She thwarts gender norms by performing both feminine and masculine duties. She subverts the meaning of pregnancy to signify a political rather than a biological process. She is, true to the Nietzschean allusion that opens this archetypal analysis, brave and unconcerned.

Athena is dressed for battle on the Burgon vase shown here, the earliest preserved Panathenaic prize amphora from 565–60 BCE.[37] She brandishes her spear and shield while

Burgon Group, *Athena wearing her aegis*, black-figured trophy amphora, c. 565 BCE, British Museum, England.

donning her aegis, a cloak made of goat skin and designed with the head of a Gorgon and its accompanying snakes. Herodotus attributes the aegis to ancient Libya, a magical site to the ancient Greeks, invoking the exotic nuance of the feminine order (the aegis is a woman's cloak). A siren appears above Athena's head, a bird-woman associated with danger and seduction, an alluring symbol of Athena's attractive potency as a female and a sign of glory, and possible peril, in battle. Athena is a dually gendered symbol of the city of Athens, a site of male strength and feminine fragility.

Athena's masculine performance of pregnancy and motherhood—the growth and birth of political valor—generates a suitable legacy for women who occupy positions of power in male spaces: figurative warriors who can operate like men. But women are not divine figures.[38] Nor do women spring *ex nihilo* from the male imaginary, though they are subject to masculine norms and ideals that archetypes like Athena and Venus personify. Women become what and who they are within a structured material reality—or a reality that suggests cognitive, linguistic, economic, and political structures. Women are (somewhat unconsciously) conditioned by these structures as they bear upon female existence: conditions of womanhood (womb) that give rise to female identities (lover and mother). They cannot flee from these conditions entirely. They cannot transcend their vexing biological functions through an exercise of reason alone. Nor can they navigate a masculine signification without social consequence. Violent Athena rises in rank, whereas violent women are swiftly marginalized, since violence is antithetical to femininity. The woman-goddess Athena, pregnant with ideas, fails to reconcile masculine political ideals and feminine (bodily) performances of womanhood. Being a woman is inherently troubling.

Women who follow in Athena's conquering footsteps do so at the expense of an assumed femininity. They are branded "aggressive" if they speak assertively and "bitchy" or "bossy" if they speak with authority, traits and behavior prized and rewarded in men. Women are labeled "emotional" if they express anger—or "on the rag," one of several crude and demeaning euphemisms for menstruation that reinforces women's bodily nature. Because the female exercise of male subjectivity threatens established gender norms, behavioral surveillance seeks to neutralize the threat of "butch" women by safeguarding femininity (and "femme" men by circumscribing masculinity). Both explicit company rules and implicit workplace norms prescribe dress and comportment.[39] Outside of work, women are expected to perform femininity through various gender-coded social activities: shopping, cleaning, cooking, baking, decorating, and so forth, contemporary equivalents of Athena's needlework and weaving. Women also devote disproportionately more time and money to the disciplining of the body to conform to feminine ideals: hair coloring, waxing, tanning, exercising, and on and on.[40]

Women who do not have children—both women who cannot conceive and/or carry a pregnancy to term and women whose relationships or values make reproduction impossible or undesirable—also find themselves locked out of Athena's reinscription of female power. They are regarded as suspect and threatening to systems of male power because women's *real power* originates in their wombs. Biological reproduction, a uniquely female, bodily function, authorizes women's economic activities and political rights, including the right to "mother" male politicians, coworkers, and colleagues by condemning or correcting their misbehavior.[41] Interestingly, women who are not yet mothers but who seek out motherhood share in Athena's warrior identity. A woman who undergoes in vitro fertilization, for instance, is thought of as someone who "fought for the pregnancy." Also, a mother whose child is bullied in school is praised for going to the administration and "fighting for her child." Fighting is a permissible facet of female identity if it is undertaken on behalf of maternal or child-rearing activities—that is, if it coheres with femininity.[42] Finally, nonchildbearing women are perceived as less authoritative than childbearing women vis-à-vis femininity.[43] Postmenopausal women with children are less threatening than childless women. But they are nonetheless considered sexually degenerative, trapped in a state of perpetual feminine decline: "not really a man but no longer a functional woman."[44]

Despite Athena's powerful performance of pregnancy as an intellectual and political exercise, she fails to normalize the professional woman or validate the childless and postmenopausal woman. Athena's promising appropriation of feminine norms—her birthing and mothering of the state—also fails to remediate the difficulties career women with children encounter, including the belief that women's professional (public) work compromises their domestic (private) responsibilities. Women professionals are often viewed as flouting gender norms because they assume historically male roles and masculine duties. Their gender identity and sexuality are evaluated with suspicion because they perform "male" duties, a suspicion that reflects the cultural exclusion of the feminine from the masculine (public and political) order.[45] Women sometimes internalize a masculine-gendered coding, which produces feelings of guilt and shame for not being available full-time to their families, especially when they are already judged for working outside of the home.[46] Even corporations and institutions that reject heteronormative and discriminatory views struggle to incorporate activities like nursing and breast-pumping into their work cultures. Family leave policies, childcare facilities, equality-minded spouses, and domestic help ease career women's work-life burdens, but these systems and support structures do not erase the threat that the masculine woman poses to men and to women themselves as they navigate shifting, gendered identity markers.[47]

Not only does Athena function outside of the procreative cycle of human life (she is a goddess), but her operations as a goddess-woman (the corporate mother) are entirely disassociated from her body: she rules not through physical strength but through mental acumen.

Her mind is pregnant with ideas. And the *birth* of her ideas, however necessary and good, undermines the unity and stability of the masculine (male-only) sphere. Athena's mythic creation reveals the primordial threat of the feminine order. Zeus claims the creation of woman for himself because the *genos gynaikōn* (race of women) in its cohesion "threatens the unity of a masculine society."[48] Major literary figures and city-states from Semonides to Euripides and from Amorgos to Athens follow suit and exclude women from Greek citizenship despite Athena's birth of the polis.[49] Excluding the female "half" from the Greek politic is a paradoxical exclusion insofar as it is "necessary and impossible at the same time."[50] In the words of Euripides's *Hippolytus*, "Zeus is responsible for the emergence of women; women are the deceitful curse, counterfeit money (*kibdēlon kakon*). They are a curse for men—that is, for all humanity, because their victims are *anthrōpoi* as a whole and not, as one might have expected, simply *andres*. They are a curse sent to earth as an act of colonization (*katoikizein*)."[51]

The conception of women in the male imaginary as a lower race or species—*gynaikōn* (womankind) as opposed to *anthropon* (humankind)—makes women hostile to the male world (they deceive, victimize, and threaten to colonize the male landscape).[52] Women's subhuman status, cursed nature, and corrupting force make female enfranchisement incompatible with (male) sociopolitical ideals. The male world neither values nor respects the feminine order and masculine order equally because of the mythic superiority of man. But the male world nonetheless needs female wombs to survive. Misogyny is the price women pay for Athena's birth from the head of her father rather than the uterus of her mother. Athena literally gives her father a migraine, symbolizing the view that woman is the source of man's pain and suffering.

The Athenian exploitation of masculine and feminine ideals sets the stage for later and more radical understandings of appropriate male and female activities. The philosophical division of self into mind and body associated with Cartesian philosophy in the seventeenth century—wherein mind is essential, and body is inessential, to selfhood—is a salient example. The subsequent gendering of Descartes's binary construction, the (productive) mind is male and the (reproductive) body is female, corresponds to the social valuing of men and women: men have greater value because they are ascribed higher "human" capacities.[53] Another example of bifurcated male and female duties is the nineteenth-century economic division of labor into disparate male and female spheres: men *work* (public, political sphere) and women *mother* (private, domestic sphere), a division that recapitulates the exclusion of the feminine in Euro-American culture.[54] Twentieth-century progressives embrace and exploit differentiated masculine and feminine activities for political purposes. Simone de Beauvoir and Betty Friedan focus on women's rational capacities and intellectual interests to resist bodily female norms like housekeeping and childbearing. They share the view that a woman's pursuit of her own intellectual interests is a necessary condition for her freedom.[55] Her body alone, the birthing and rearing of humans, could never serve to liberate or complete her. The cultural repression of femininity calls us to retheorize human subjectivity and redesign the world to value body and mind equally.

Athena as Woman

Athena's sex alone does not mark her masculine comportment toward the world as deviant: classical Greek women were able to assume male duties.[56] But even in cultures with pronounced examples of gender fluidity, human sexuality is mapped onto social and biological systems that stabilize what it means to be male and female. Men and women are treated as natural and opposing categories. Male-female opposition generates an ideology of gender that normalizes masculine and feminine expressions and activities. Men are rational, active, and assertive, masculine traits that define male behavior and biological functions. Women are emotional (irrational), passive, and submissive, feminine traits that define female behavior and biological functions. The presumptive rationality of men, understood as a positive, intellectual activity of the mind, is considered antithetical to the bodily activity of female reproduction, a presumably abject, passive process. Athena's masculine identity may enhance her competitiveness among male gods and instantiate a prescient model of gender subversion, but her failure to perform femininity, *her lack of physical reproductivity,* ironically undermines the female subjectivity she so powerfully exemplifies.[57]

Athena may be wise to suspend her womb for the sake of civic engagement. Her action exposes the Western tradition's two-sphere system of human activity (public and private) for differently sexed bodies. Public activities, civic and financial leadership among them, enjoy especially high value in a two-sphere context. Public activities are also highly gendered since they rely on citizens, an exclusively male group, for financial support and fulfillment (private, female activities do not implicate the polis since they are funded through private family resources). Women's access to the public sphere is therefore contingent on female ties to male privilege. Their ability to buy their way into religious and political activities exemplifies the economic and social advancement of women through marriage and family, a practice that persists in contemporary cultures. The economic value of public activities and their correlative prestige elevates the male sphere above the female sphere. Without money and a sphere of their own, women lack the means to signify feminine activities as valued, social goods.

Women's symbolic sacrifice of childbearing for masculine power transcends the ancient world. Pressures to perform in *exclusively* masculine or feminine ways compel women to choose between home and work, husband and boss, children and career. Feminist work has clearly improved the experience and status of women in the public sphere. Women's access to education and opportunities for economic advancement are equitable to men's in most contemporary societies. But private, domestic obligations remain insufficiently reformed.

Repression of feminine identities in Western culture, read as both a bodily phenomenon and a discursive category. Feminine repression recurs in cultural narratives, social structures, religious practices, and political-judicial systems.[58] Greek sexuality operates within a one-sex vertical system of biological sex with the male sex at the top of the hierarchy.[59] Classical figures regard the female body as a derivation of the male standard and utilize the single-sexed, two-gendered system to honor the father above the mother.[60] The *use* of bodies serves to situate differences between men and women: women birth babies. The use of women's bodies also plays a highly significant role in the valuing of their bodies.[61] Ancient women serve in prominent, religious roles as cult worship priestesses, caregivers of the temple (house) of cult statues, an analogous function to the caregiving they provide in private domestic spaces (cleaning, washing, decorating, weaving, and cooking).[62] The use of female bodies for public religious rituals helps codify Greek constructions of femininity in antiquity.[63] Caring for others is constitutive of femininity. Women's so-called caring (biologically constituted) nature includes reproduction. Young women of ancient Greece could serve in virgin priesthoods as temple figures and caregivers for a short time. But lifelong virginity—an example set by Herakles as a punishment of Thespius's daughter who rejects him—is considered disgraceful as it violates feminine behavioral codes.[64] Even the wise, conquering Athena cannot escape female bodily norms entirely.

This example of a late Archaic black-figure amphora depicts the judgment of Paris. Fragmentary sources of the story, later elaborated by Ovid, narrate a battle for beauty among Aphrodite, Hera, and Athena. In this ancient beauty contest, the three goddesses irritate Zeus by fighting over who is the prettiest. Zeus appoints Paris as the judge to choose a winner and end the debate. Here Hermes, with his winged shoes and caduceus, leads Hera, Athena, and Aphrodite to Paris for judgment. True to their goddess nature, they negotiate with Paris to ensure a win: each offers a gift as a manifestation of her individual beauty. Hera, goddess of marriage and women, offers to make Paris king of all men; Athena, goddess of wisdom and war, promises him victory in battle; and Aphrodite, goddess of beauty, love, and procreation, promises Paris the hand of Helen of Troy,

The Group of Würzburg, *Judgment of Paris*, black-figured amphora, c. 510 BCE, Museum of Fine Arts, Boston, U.S.A.

the most beautiful woman in the world. Paris selects Aphrodite, sealing women's fate as sexual and reproductive creatures and initiating the Trojan War, a representation of woman's power as lover.

Athena dutifully refuses marriage and maternity for herself but presides over these life-giving practices for Athens, exemplifying the value of self-sacrifice.[65] She exploits masculine identity to wrest power away from male gods, but the polis she creates never fully distinguishes the women of Athens from the goddess.[66] Athena's legacy of the womb—a birthing of ideas, a performance of (masculine) intellectual labor—does not bear out for the women who worship her. Even when female figures transcend the domestic sphere, their authority and subjectivity remain vested in their bodily form and labor. Women's value resides *in the biological use of the womb* particularly.

While the hierarchical privileging of masculinity drives the Greek repression of the feminine order, bodies bear different meanings in changing social and political circumstances.[67] Enlightenment-era discourse reconstitutes the meaning of opposing bodies in a two-sex construct: males and females are opposite *sexes* with irreducible differences (fundamental types rather than degrees of difference). The male-female binary is codified in the eighteenth century as an ontological category.[68] Men and women are *by nature* different and distinct, a division reinforced by Cartesian mind-body dualism that gives rise to modern systems of meaning.[69] Although we now admit the limitations and oversimplifications of the male/masculine and female/

feminine disjunction, this disjunction persists in the West's collective cultural imagination.

Bodies represent and mirror sexual differences. But bodies alone do not situate sexed identity. Pregnancy makes visible the shifting configurations of bodies and their cultural meanings—for example, pregnant bodies signify the gap between sex (flesh) and gender (ideology).[70] Wombs signify varied understandings of femininity: religious, political, libidinous, and aesthetic. The activities female bodies are expected to perform, the disciplining and coding of embodied female activities as feminine, normalize the disjunction between femininity and masculinity. Archetypal uses of women's bodies—for reproduction, comfort and protection, sexual gratification, and aesthetic pleasure—reinforce the extant privileging of masculine over feminine performances of subjectivity. Athena's performance of motherhood, her birthing of the polis, authorizes the privileging of the masculine order, an order that seeks comfort in the feminine sphere. Contemporary women nurture children *and* careers: they have private and public responsibilities. But the implicit logic of the disjunction and the underlying structure of the community in which the disjunction is embedded resist women's movements between feminine and masculine spheres of action. Many social and economic barriers to women's equality are rooted in the denigration of the suppressed feminine, bodily order.

Athena's archetype of woman does little to help women with careers and families embody coherent self-identities. Her subversion of the feminine order destabilizes the female subject in both public and private spheres. But contemporary applications of Athena's pregnant subjectivity—the metaphor of womb as political space—show that Athena's womb is not her own. Even if the average woman never invokes Athena by name, she knows intimately the reality Athena manifests in the world: femininity is a bodily performance, and reproduction is its central act.

Feminist Engagement with the Political Womb

Athena's representative elevation of mind over body resonates with modern feminist ideals. Eradicating (or controlling) the female reproductive cycle creates an opening for female choice, a distancing of the bodily roles and connotations historically attached to womanhood—a belief in inherent female traits such as physical weakness, natural emotionality, and instinctive nurturing. The privileging of mind also energizes feminist politics. Olympe de Gouges in France and Mary Wollstonecraft in Great Britain, together with their Enlightenment allies, argue that women are rational creatures and, by virtue of their rationality, deserve political rights as an expression of their equality with men. Whereas de Gouges attributes women's inequality to a lack of protected civil freedoms, Wollstonecraft argues that women's slavish education has crippled their bodies and minds, impeding women's capacity to achieve equality with men. Their calls for gender equality and social transformation (for the benefit of everyone) have shaped the rhetoric of women's rights in subsequent ages.

Twentieth- and twenty-first-century platforms for women's rights reflect medical advances of these eras. In both cases, freedom is seen as developing women's rational capacities rather than elevating or reconceiving their reproductive capacities. In fact, reproductive control in the form of protected reproductive rights (access to birth control, abortion services, maternity leave, and the right to work while pregnant) is arguably the defining issue of second-wave feminism, a feminism of "choice." The rhetoric of choice implies that female freedom—freedom to work, freedom to have children (or not)—resides in the activity of the womb. To be free is to decide whether and/or when to have or not have children. Hence freedom for women—intellectual, economic, social, and political—is defined by the female body.

Second-wave feminism and liberal understandings of freedom as self-sovereignty have an important place in an exploration of pregnant subjectivity. But the implication that women's freedom *requires* restrictions of bodily operations rather than a restructuring of the sociopolitical world bears reexamination. Though the mind is embodied alike for men and women, women's bodies alone nourish and bear children, activities that temporarily reduce women's capacities for work (political and economic labor). Because work, a historically masculine activity, has high value, any reduction in work capacity is viewed negatively. Thus the female body, an impediment to rational thought and (male) productivity, must be managed, controlled, even erased from the modern world. Ironically, the modern feminist push for greater educational and economic opportunities for women facilitates the signification of the womb as political space.

Athena's lack of fertility intensifies rather than eases the female burden given our inherited conceptions and narratives of womanhood. On the Christian account, the Holy Spirit entrusts Mary to birth a divine savior. She is physically connected to the divinity of her child: some readings stress the generation of Christ's blood, bone, and flesh within Mary's body.[71] Her nursing breast so prominently displayed in the *Maria lactans* (the nursing Madonna) imagery reflects a positive understanding of the body in Christian faith: "from the earliest days of Christianity, 'the virgin's nursing breast, the lactating virgin, was the primary symbol of God's love for humanity.'"[72] Though Mary also gives rational assent to her pregnancy—she says yes to God—she may not "own" her womb in ways that enlightened readers would recognize. She nonetheless births a child *and* a church. Her production in body and spirit exemplifies a unified rather than divided mind and body. Mary models, at least in modest form, embodied, coherent agency. Ironically, she contributes to the formation of a robust female subjectivity that pregnancy advances.

Reconceiving Athena

Recognizing the body, female and male, as a territory to explore marks a transition from a mystical to a scientific understanding of human nature. By bracketing the reproductive function of the female body, Athena neutralizes its presumed negative value just as Mary's virginity provides positive value to feminine reproduction by counterbalancing the image of Eve as the first and worst sinner (women are the cause of sexual sin according to traditional Old Testament exegesis). Women's bodies, when read within an Athenian paradigm, share in the same value system as men's bodies and, thus, may be dissected and studied without scandal or special signification. Though it is right to reject the supposition of the male body as the human ideal and resist practices that force women to assume a masculine subject position, the scientific interest in the female body in the seventeenth and eighteenth centuries helpfully contributes to a recognition of women's nonreproductive capacities, including their rational capacities. It also promotes the rapid advancement of obstetrics.[73] The creation of anatomical atlases and illustrations represents a full-fledged spatial understanding of the body, one that was facilitated by the economic idea of commodity that first emerged in relation to divine relics. Conceived as a remote and unknown aspect of the self, a source of chaos and uncertainty, the body was portrayed by artists and scholars as a threatening landmass.[74] As Western empires begin to colonize foreign lands for political gain, modern literature and art attempt to colonize the body itself.[75] In keeping with this aesthetic trend, artists skillfully map the practices of land expansion onto human cadavers in their depictions of anatomical study.[76] Their images suggest that unless the body is claimed, conquered, and controlled by scientific tools and political weaponry, its volatile nature will destroy the social order and prevent political growth.

Athena's promising archetype of pregnant subjectivity, an archetype that offers women new exercises of agency by legitimating varieties of productivity, remains abject in the face of feminine, bodily, biological birth. Woman is, in the shadow of Athena, an empty category. Constructs of femininity, expositions of what it means to be a woman ontologically, empirically, and discursively, bind together biology and society. Robust female subjectivity necessitates a phenomenology of transcendence *with body* instead of transcendence *of body*—that is, a resignification rather than suspension of immanent, bodily, feminine, *wombed* activities even if the female body is never deployed for reproductive purposes.[77]

The Athenian move away from the deeply bodily Mary divests the womb of its social and political import. Yet biological reproduction need not be a woman's singular contribution to civic life. Hannah Arendt aligns women with the labor of the home and men with the action of the polis. Implicit in Arendt's account is that for women to become active in political life, they must eschew having children (as she herself did) and become like men.[78] Athena's radical reimaging of motherhood as a political practice creates the possibility for women to pursue something beyond, or in addition to, biological motherhood. Women may gain operational parity with men—same degrees, same jobs, same pay. But equality will elude even enlightened societies so long as the public and political spheres are designed for male bodies and masculine identities alone. The reproduction of flesh and the production of ideas continue to oppose one another.

Athena is not disembodied; she is functionally male, a sign of the repression of feminine subjectivity in civic life. Her body signifies the city-state she represents and foreshadows the modern politicization of human bodies: bodies as territories to map, colonize, and conquer in the name of civilization. The choice between children and career, private and public roles, is not a mythic one. Jobs demand trade-offs. With all due homage to Athena and the female oppression she resists, feminists must conquer Athena too. For wisdom to truly be a warrior, feminists must challenge the passive, abject, and biological signification of pregnant subjectivity without denying the powerful, biological structures that condition womanhood. Venus provides a provocative move in this direction by freeing female sexuality from a strictly biological role. Venus normalizes sex for physical pleasure and emotional connection. Her expanded view of female fertility signifies womb as erotic space.

3

Subduing Venus

Womb as Erotic Space

For men to be instructed, they must
be seduced by aesthetics.
—Arnaud-Eloi Gautier d'Agoty

Venus materializes nearly out of thin air amid a sea of
Roman gods and goddesses. She bears an elemental, one
might say *earthy*, relationship to the material world. As an
ancient Italian goddess of spring, she represents vegetal
fertility and rebirth.[1] Her associations with gardens, vines,
and myrtles signify her primary identification with regeneration. Her tie to the land gives way to a later association

with the sea when she is transformed by the Romans into the Greek Aphrodite's counterpart, a Latin goddess of love, sex, and reproduction.[2]

Venus's transition from horticultural to human propagation entails a harrowing origin story. The sex goddess surfaces after Saturn (Cronus or Cronos) castrates his father, Caelus (Uranus or Ouranos), and flings the severed phallus into the ocean. The phallus skips across the water, scattering bloody seafoam as it goes. Venus arises naked and radiant, a seductive love-mate on the half shell: a feminine paragon without protection.[3] She is vulnerable and defenseless—she lacks Mary's spiritual fidelity and Athena's intellectual prowess—but her looks subdue rather than enflame men. She exploits her aesthetic appeal to direct male desire away from power and toward productive ends; she copulates with men, performing a symbolic act of castration that subdues the threat of death.[4] She thus transcends the gruesome violence that marks her beginning by inciting attraction, ecstasy, and procreation.[5] Venus's sexualized performance of female subjectivity authorizes an erotic coding of womb that opposes women's idealized repression yet encourages women's objectification.[6]

Venus as Civilizing Force

The Roman goddess of love is a predictable archetype of the pregnant subject. Venus shores up the causal link between sexual intercourse and pregnancy by birthing more than a dozen children. Her romantic overtures tie together sex and love: she is the mother of the winged Cupids (*Erotes*). She ignites sexual energy for pleasure and procreation. She tamps down sexual energy when it threatens to spill over and wreck the political order of the day. Her oversight of Eros runs the gamut of the sexual spectrum from chastity to promiscuity. As *Venus Verticordia* (changer of hearts), she cultivates virginity by directing desire toward procreation, a sublimating act that invites comparison to Mary. Her management of reproduction also strikes a strong Athenian note. Venus is an imperial deity for whom sexuality serves the state (sex facilitates economic and familial prosperity through marriage and children). Lawful citizens, whose status sex engenders, ensure military victory, a value *Venus Victrix* (bringer of victory), like Athena, endorses. Though Venus rejects chastity herself—she enjoys sex with gods and mortals— she shares Athena's honor of birthing the political realm: she is the mother of Aeneas, founder of Rome, who survives the fall of Troy and flees to Italy.[7] The mother-goddess's biological role in the formation of the state fixes her feminine attribution, an attribution Athena, a metaphoric mother, enjoys only marginally. Julius Caesar claims Venus as his ancestor and integrates her into Roman religious life. His temple (46 BCE) was dedicated to *Venus Genetrix* (begetting mother). Adoration of the mother is a legacy Mary and Venus share. Venus blesses and safeguards growing wombs and wards off labor pains.[8]

Despite the archetypal similarities among Mary, Athena, and Venus, their performances of pregnancy bear a radical difference. *Venus is a sexualized mother.* Her integration of sexual desire into the female psyche separates her from the pure, virginal Mary and the chaste, rational Athena. Whereas Mary and Athena suspend their sexual desire to produce external social order, Venus concentrates her desire on the interior human landscape.[9] She alone codifies the affective, psychosocial functions of sex—physical, emotional, and psychological attachments between partners and their loving integration into civic structures and family systems. She reframes sex as a spiritual *practice* as opposed to a passive spiritual *process* as in the Marian example.[10] She shows that sexual arousal can produce states of erotic and religious ecstasy that facilitate transcendence from despair. Her personal coupling and reproducing children with gods and men substantiate her spiritual worldview.[11]

Venus deploys sexual desire to alleviate psychic anxiety, specifically existential dread and despair, a function that appears to grow naturally out of her disordered roots. The catharsis generated through sexual intercourse eases perennial concerns about mortality and finitude—human fears of rejection, alienation, and death—through bonding and regeneration.[12] Venus fittingly mothers Timor (Phobos), who personifies fear; his twin brother, Metus (Deimos), who personifies terror; and Concordia (Harmonia), a daughter who personifies concord and harmony. Venus's subjectivity also lays bare the psychological effects of embodied femininity. Utilizing women's bodies to birth or bolster masculine systems of power bends the female psyche toward submission. Treating wombs as male spaces, however we mark them (sacred, political, erotic, material, or other), deprives women of meaningful autonomy and dignity.

Female archetypes of womanhood operate as valuable heuristics in women's reimagination of self. Icons exemplify negative and positive valences of female experience: patriarchy dictating women's identities and women subverting patriarchy. Treating wombs as female spaces invites women to resist cultural imaginings of womanhood, expand the idea and experience of wombed personhood, and secure the authority to reshape constructs of femininity. Treating wombs as female spaces—spaces that are also desirable and valuable to others, spaces that expand and contract as women share their (pro)creative work with the world- -makes possible women's integration into civic activities. Signifying wombs as female spaces legitimates women's influence in male affairs and invites women into generative personal, social, and political practices. Viewing wombs as female spaces frees women to shape the structural spaces that circumscribe their lives and pursue projects that transcend their embodied situations.

Believing that women exist primarily to perpetuate male success and happiness normalizes male dominance. Venus cleverly deploys the womb to civilize the brutality of the male world, a mutually psychological and spiritual function. Sex transforms isolated, desperate, and dying individuals into subdued couples bound together eternally by their reproduction of biological descendants.[13] Appropriating the womb as a therapeutic device also enables Venus to transcend her degrading past.[14] Venus's birth from an inseminated sea casts her as a polluted product of passion and pain.[15] In this example of a fifth-century BCE relief, she displays her exposed breasts and abdomen, conventional erogenous zones, to arouse her audience's desire for fertilizing unions.[16] Rather than cover her bosom with her arms—as is typical of Marian iconography once the breast becomes erotically charged—she daringly exposes her bare torso by extending her arms upward, reaching for her mother, the sky, a symbol of her feminine lineage.[17] Saturn disrupts Venus's matrilineal horizon when he castrates his father, Caelus, a punishment for abusing his mother that allows Caelus to assume the birthing process for himself and convey Venus's sexualized signification and function (she is born from his genitals).[18] As female attendants lift Venus out of the sea, they reclaim her as a daughter of the sky and distance her from the masculine world that births her. She clings to these celestial, female

The Ludovisi Throne, marble, c. 470 BCE, National Roman Museum, Italy.

figures, a sign of her mutual reclamation of their collective femininity. But she does not *and cannot*, given her responsibility for fertility, leave the male world entirely. Civilization entails biological proliferation in Venus's field of meaning and cannot be merely a male undertaking despite Athena's remarkable counterexample.[19] Earthly and human propagation in the Venus schema turns on woman's capacity to subdue man's disposition toward dominance. Female sexual agency, acquired through an appropriation of male power, facilitates human civilization. Venus's eroticism is salvific rather than incriminating.

The artistic separation of Venus's head (thought) and genitalia (desire) in the Ludovisi Throne's marble relief symbolizes the opposing—and, in her world, *conflictual*—masculine and feminine orders.[20] She aspires to rouse men and women to resolve their battles by physically uniting and subduing their divergent potencies, ultimately ensuring civilization's continuation through offspring. The inherent gender duality of human procreation is suggested by the undulating folds covering her lower body. The carved cloth replicates water, connoting Venus's masculine birth, and emulates a vaginal opening, symbolizing Venus's envisaged feminine birth. Venus's birth symbolizes the necessary encoding and harmonizing of male and female signs on which civilization depends. She is, appropriately, the mother of Hermaphroditus.

Human birth re-creates vestiges of Venus's birth. A fetus grows within a placenta filled with amniotic fluid, a liquid womb that recalls the sea from which Venus springs.

A physician pulls the fetus from its watery home and, like Venus's female attendants, lifts the infant into the light of life, a nod to Venus's gaze upon her mother, sky. The child fuses mother and father equally, binding and renewing their withering spirits. The mother and father are symbolically reborn through the child who makes possible their eternal life (through descendants) even in the light of their mortality.[21] Reproduction serves as a tangible sign of the civilizing power of sex.

Venus as Androgynous Womb

Attempts to bind the masculine and feminine orders in equal measure break down over the assumed meaning, purpose, and power of woman's womb. Athena, for instance, suppresses her femininity and adopts a masculine subject position to acquire male power. Athena is a crafty and wise warrior-goddess. Her mothering of the polis with her armored body and strong mind codes womb as political space. Venus, by contrast, exaggerates her femininity and, true to her family lineage, castrates (by copulating and procreating with) men and male gods, a power play that also differentiates her from the virginal Mary whose asexual insemination by the Holy Spirit codes womb as sacred space. Mary is a pure and faithful Holy Mother. Venus's subduing of man through sexual sublimation and regeneration civilizes the masculine order and codes womb as erotic space. Venus is a lusty, assertive, and feminine love goddess.

Venus's archetypal performance of pregnancy moves beyond the Mary-Athena binary. She, like Mary, carries and births children, human and divine. She, like Athena, embodies and births civic ideals, such as unity between men and women. But the effervescent Venus, with her *bodily, erotic* reproduction of people, ideas, and emotions, grounds female agency in a sexual activity instead of a social role. She shifts the Marian-Athenian focus of embodied female identity from mother to lover. Venus thus enters logically into a genealogy of pregnancy after Mary and Athena, who perform pregnancy nonsexually.[22]

The principal reading of Mary is as a nonagential (submissive), nondesiring (asexual), feminine (relational) subject. She signifies woman as mother and womb as sacred space. Mary performs pregnancy as an untouched, untainted, vessel whose sacred obligation is to discharge God's call to reproduce and realize God's providential design for the human world. Athena presents as a highly agential (assertive), nondesiring (asexual), and masculine (autonomous) pregnant subject. She signifies woman as warrior and womb as political space. Athena performs pregnancy as a wise, militaristic ruler who suspends her feminine capacities to access the masculine order, craft ideas, and birth political structures. Venus is represented as an agential (assertive), desiring (sexual), and feminine (relational) subject. She signifies woman as lover and womb as erotic space. Venus performs pregnancy as an alluring goddess who uses her sex appeal to sublimate male aggression, subdue psychic angst, and unite men and women through sexual intimacy and reproduction. As the chapter titles declare, *Mary delivers, Athena conquers,* and *Venus subdues* the masculine order. They mother, order, and harmonize the male world, respectively, through their uniquely signified and performed wombed activities.

Venus's harmonizing work extends to reproductivity itself: she treats sex and procreation as dually sacred (Marian) *and* civilizing (Athenian) activities. By inscribing pregnancy with religious and political meaning, Venus effectively marries Mary's feminine and Athena's masculine performances of female subjectivity. Similarly, her signification of womb as erotic space powerfully unites women and men in the shared project of childbirth and suggests a more equitable distribution of power around childcare roles. Venus's unification of feminine and masculine signs also frees couples to reimagine their embodied identities by challenging the gender breakdown and coding of parental activities and responsibilities and perhaps progressing further by developing an appreciation for nonbinary and transgender subject positions and power relations.[23] Her invitation to envision and embody alternative configurations of heteronormativity through coupling and child-rearing activities makes her an apt and valuable contributor to gender and identity politics.

Venus exerts additional progressive force by dissolving the normative division of motherhood into feminine (Mary) and masculine (Athena) modes of reproductivity. By subduing masculine dominance, she embodies desire *and* agency, a feminine (relational) expression of male power. Her androgynous signification of motherhood appeals to progressives who seek to challenge traditional parenting practices. Adoptive mothers, cisgender biological mothers, foster mothers, godmothers, "house mothers," nonbinary biological mothers, and transgender biological mothers are all welcomed and affirmed as "mothers" under Venus's androgynous banner. Male and female lovers will, given their varied sexual and gender identities, unite and perform masculine and feminine signs in diverse ways and, thus, embody pregnancy and reproduction differently. Venus's instantiation of the erotic womb as a shared space subject to changing significations makes room for diverse (literal and figurative) pregnancies that cumulatively serve to quiet the psyche and spirit, unify men and women, and ultimately civilize human affairs through love.

Venus as Sexual Icon

Popular audiences are endlessly fascinated with the love goddess. Her enduring attraction arises from her commanding vision for human intimacy. Apart from her continued cultural relevance for understanding and shaping female agency and identity, Venus captures the aesthetic imagination of artists. She attracts audiences across Europe and North America in the late eighteenth and early nineteenth centuries who are inspired by the rise of neoclassicism and upper-class affinities. Viewings of Hellenistic and Renaissance examples of the idealized female figure appear on the "Grand Tour" of continental Europe: Botticelli's *Birth of Venus* (1482–85), Titian's *Venus of Urbino* (1538), and the *Venus de' Medici* (first century BCE) among them.[24]

Beneath her facade of ordered beauty and physical perfection, Venus symbolizes sexual desire as a painful irritant in desperate need of relief that she can, if deployed, provide through living women and their wombs. In this peristyle of the eponymously named *House of Venus in the Shell* in Pompeii, she represents *transfigured desire* as a pearl, a highly prized gemstone formed painstakingly from grit within the soft tissue of a living animal.[25] Sexual longing is like the grain that becomes a pearl: it penetrates and permeates the body, creates agonizing pain, and enjoys relief upon its transformation and release from the body. Expressed more prosaically, erotic desire overtakes and tortures men who pursue relief through the penetrating act of intercourse and climax that culminates in a magnificent child who the man loves and protects.

The *Venus Anadyomeme* fresco captures the impending process of transfiguration (the sex act itself) that Venus inspires: an aroused penis, suggested by the vertical staff on the left, looms over Venus's soft, open vaginal bed supported by a winged Cupid, a symbol of desire, on the right.

Venus anadyomeme, fresco from the House of Venus, c. 100 CE.

Her jewelry, particularly her crown, represents her sacred and imperial authority. But her naked body alone—*without armor, thunderbolt, or Trident for symbolic reinforcement*—is the source of her power, instantiating woman as lover. The blue water and sky framing the fresco represent her father, the sea, and mother, the sky. She is positioned between her two parents whose opposition she lovingly unites.

Venus's aesthetic power over people represents human vulnerability in the face of overpowering desire. Her beauty draws together men and women who unite in sexual ecstasy to transcend the pain of life.[26] Her safeguarding of sex's spiritual and civic functions nurtures a robust intimacy that expands pregnancy beyond its familial limits. Venus's paradigm of female subjectivity, marked by a subversion of gender roles, expands pregnancy beyond its material limits. Female wombs grow and bear children to civilize the male world; female minds create and express (birth) ideas to equalize power across social orders. Gender performativity takes on new meaning in light of Venus's archetypal woman.

But sex has lost the spiritual import and civic force it once enjoyed. People have arranged their lives to avoid vulnerability. Desire, so easily gratified, no longer overwhelms the body or threatens the psyche. Sexual transcendence from pain and despair has been rendered absurd. The resulting impoverishment of intimacy, typified by the opposing extremes of utilitarian and pornographic views of sexual encounters as well as conflicting hypermedicalized and overtrivialized conceptions of pregnancy, depletes desire of its harmonizing power.

Desirous women are not exactly men's playthings as Wollstonecraft fears.[27] Neither are they passive wombs as Beauvoir claims.[28] Or defiled slits, holes, or openings as Dworkin prophesizes.[29] They are, though, *like* dolls, *like* wombs, *like* holes within the erotic poles of popular culture: sensual objects produced by the paradoxical demands of aesthetic allure and sexual propriety (and reproduced by ever-changing conceptions of female sexuality). The incoherence of a female sexual subject—of an openly *desiring* and *desirous* woman who regards sex as dually sacred (Marian) and civilizing (Athenian)—grows along with the expanding variables of sexuality.[30] Burgeoning sexuality scholars in the mid-twentieth century theorized sex as the primary link between biological and psychic structures of personhood.[31] Venus aptly represents (and facilitates) this imagined, ecstatic, and subduing fusion of body and mind, a "happy reunion with destiny."[32] Yet the process of becoming a modern, female sexual subject—an active, autonomous, sexually subjugating creature—is fraught despite the denial of many sex-positive feminists. Women are compelled to navigate contradictory ideals and prohibitions that undermine healthy, self-directing performances of female sexuality. They must negotiate an objectifying male gaze that claims the psychosocial process of desire formation for itself.[33]

Venus's subduing power over masculine domination is rendered impotent in the context of women's *Otherness*. Disciplinary practices of femininity socialize women to discipline their bodies and desires to conform to man's surveilling judgment of attractiveness and desirability.[34] Women thus subject their bodies to feminizing practices that increase male sexual desire, such as dieting and exercising, as well as surgical modifications.[35] Because male pleasure so completely circumscribes female sexuality, women see themselves through male norms of desirability. Women even construe themselves as sexual objects rather than desiring subjects, which orients the female psyche toward submission.[36] Women also reformulate male desire as female desire: they experience arousal when men are aroused by them.[37] The totalizing effect of the male gaze on the female body is the complete structural and material subordination of woman subjects. Evidence of this totalizing effect is that every part of a woman's body, *including her womb*, and all her embodied experiences, *including pregnancy*, are eroticized by the male gaze.

Venus prefigures the feminist suggestion that eroticizing motherhood—dissolving the separation between motherhood and sexuality—might liberate women from male oppression.[38] Yet eroticizing pregnancy ignores divergent constructions of desire and operations of power. Milk-engorged breasts become objects for male pleasure rather than sources of physical (or spiritual, as in the case of Mary) nourishment once desire is introduced into the scheme of pregnancy. And breasts become subject to social discipline: public breastfeeding is prohibited or restricted to specified spaces like nursing rooms. Sexualizing the pregnant body also decenters women from reproductive processes so that men, like Zeus and Caelus before them, can control reproduction themselves. The active male is represented as saving the passive female from infertility by penetrating her distressed, damsel egg with his valiant, whip-like sperm, a mirroring of the male penetration of the female body in sexual intercourse.[39] Sexualizing pregnancy perpetuates masculine norms of womanhood by transforming women into passive objects for male cultural consumption rather than subjects of female experience.[40] Once the pregnant body is sexually charged, the womb becomes a zone of male entry, pleasure, and control.[41] Finally, eroticizing pregnancy reinforces reproduction as a bodily phenomenon and dissuades women from refusing pregnancy (they give up authority if they defy their "natural" female activities, an activity they themselves may have internalized as normal) *or* reconceptualizing pregnancy as a figurative process of embodied, intellectual productivity.[42]

Women may seek to restore Venus's paradigm of womanhood through reconstituted conceptions of intimacy and transfigured representations of sex. But retheorizing sex as a harmonizing exercise—an authentic act of human intersubjectivity—will not free women from the male gaze. Man's delight in woman's beautiful body and growing bump does not erase the erotic taint of the female.[43] No bodily zone or experience refuses the penetrating male gaze.

Venus as Tainted Womb

Motherhood has served as a woman's primary historic pathway out of structural subordination and political oppression.

Birthing a child absolves her from the sin of being born a woman because using her womb "as intended," fulfilling the uterus's biological capacity and embodying codified norms of femininity, revalues the female body as good. The positive personal, social, and political efficacy of female regeneration explains why women who are not mothers threaten the male world: they subvert the biological process for recapitulating male power. Although Venus nicely expands the performance of femininity beyond biological motherhood—*her desired aim is male-female harmony across social orders*—her bodily, erotic signification of the female sex continues to subjugate and subordinate women in the Western cultural imagination.

Ideological constructions of motherhood track with Mary (mother as caregiver) and Athena (mother as protector) rather than Venus (mother as lover). In fact, mothers, ideologically speaking, do not have sex: they are, like Mary and Athena, pure and chaste. Venus could help us recover a conception of pregnancy that elevates the experience and agency of mothering persons and the reproductive labor, real and metaphoric, they perform: a sacred rather than erotic ecstasy.[44] Sex's sacred coding sanctions women's rejection of sexual repression, which subjugates the mind and body, as well as sexual promiscuity, which cheapens sexual encounters.[45] But even the sacralization of sex serves to subjugate female desire to a procreative function and prescribes parenthood as a sacred duty. It also treats woman as a Marian vehicle for male religious transcendence. Though the religious signification of sexuality normalizes sexual activity as a positive good—*sex has the power to elicit grace and, from a Christian perspective, inscribe bodies and the children they produce with divinity*—it also reinforces a signification of woman as evil.[46] Even Venus's womb is tainted.

Venus as Woman

The goddess Venus assumes the ontology of an actual object, a doll no less, when museums and medical schools appropriate her identity as a motif for stylized wax mannequins and ivory figurines.[47] These anatomized and dissectible female figures, many of them pregnant, are made of wood, ivory, or wax. They are designed to teach and enchant the viewer, serving to lure men into learning, a testament to the veracity of Arnaud-Eloi Gautier d'Agoty's epigraphic comments that men must be seduced into learning by aesthetics.[48] The allusion to Venus is apt given the contemporaneous popularity of the love goddess as a subject for artistic representation. Leopold II, the Grand Duke of Tuscany (1747–92), sought to civilize his subjects by illustrating empirically observable natural laws in human anatomy, a perfect reflection of the orderly workings of the larger natural world.[49] Students would arrange, touch, and manipulate the organs and fetuses inside these figures in lieu of live cadavers. He appointed his court physician Felice Fontana (1730–1805) to oversee the creation of female models for use as props for medical school instructions as well as the museums in which they were subsequently displayed.[50] Fontana's aim was to make cadaver dissection obsolete by producing an encyclopedia of the human body in wax form and to sanitize the learning process by creating "permanent, odour-free, and incorruptible" cadavers.[51] He failed in his mission but contributed to the growth of anatomical science and its accompanying desacralization of the body.

Through his revolutionary dissections, Andreas Vesalius (1514–64), the father of modern anatomy, suggests that "only by understanding the dead body can we hope to understand the living."[52] This intriguing suggestion is more than poetic musing. Legal acts written between the sixteenth and eighteenth centuries codified penal dissection to meet the demands of justice and the needs of science. Despite its pragmatic beginnings, dissection satisfies more than utilitarian ends. If, as Vesalius suggests, the body is a field of inquiry, a source and site of meaning, then dissection is an epistemological endeavor. The Y-incision—a Y-shaped cut made from shoulder to shoulder meeting at the breastbone and extending all the way down to the pubic bone to open up the breastplate of a corpse and gain access to the body's major organs—aids with "enculturating the body as text. . . . The Y-incision opens the book, authorizing the readability of an interior structure available to the pathologist as the discourse of (Western) disease."[53]

Like the dissector who reads bodies according to their physiological functions and anatomical structures, audiences in performance venues observe bodies "for the purpose of constructing meaning."[54] Reading bodies as text—probing and interpreting a body's hidden structures—invests both the reader and the bodies with agency and authority.[55] This means that anatomized bodies, real and figurative, become knowable subjects "both in the sense of being *subjected*—of being isolated and disempowered—and of being <u>subjected</u>—imagined to be endowed with qualities of intention and subjectivity."[56]

The subjection of the female body registers as literal in the case of wax models categorized as the Anatomical Venus.[57] Wax is eerily "similar in appearance to human flesh."[58] Consider this famous 1782 life-size dissectible *Venerina* (Little Venus), a wax model created by Clemente Susini in Bologna, Italy, one of countless examples of anatomical dolls associated with Venus.[59] If one ignores Venerina's flayed state—if the model were clothed, for instance—one might see a female figure in repose. The figure's placement in a familiar domestic scene softens the reality she represents: a deceased woman and fetus. "Wax models . . . were posed as if alive" and "pain-free" to distance the viewers from "the contemplation of death and bloody internal organs," an impossibility when working with cadavers (and

Clemente Susini, *Venerina* (Little Venus), life-sized dissectible wax model, 1782. Courtesy of Museo di Palazzo Poggi—Università di Bologna, Italy.

deeply ironic in this context, given Venus's very bloody and painful origin story).[60]

From 1825 to 1900, Londoners enjoyed at least one Anatomical Venus in circulation. A provocative example of an Anatomical Venus is the automatized *Sleeping Venus* whose breast rises and falls subtly "as if she were alive."[61] The Venus trope provides a legitimating frame for viewing the taboo naked female body. In reality, anatomical discourse well into the twentieth century excludes women's bodies from study and discussion, with the exception of obstetrics, because the male body is regarded as "the 'universal' anatomical model."[62] The Anatomical Venus thus operates as a subterfuge for gazing at nude female figures. On a deeper, psychic level, the Anatomical Venus revives the spiritual and civilizing elements of sexuality and love suppressed by rationalist exertions of order and control. She recognizes the power of erotic love to resolve the existential threat of death. The Anatomical Venus also calls forth the unconscious idea that the feminine and masculine orders are unifiable through practices of intimacy that produce intersubjectivity.[63]

Venus's transformation from a mythological subject and art object to a modern teaching tool and titillating doll warrants further examination.[64] One can understand why students of science would prefer wax models to cadavers (wax models lack bodily fluids and odors). But the appropriation of the love goddess's identity for dissectible wax dolls inscribes an idealized, eroticized femininity onto the female body that undermines women's subjectivity:

inanimate dolls lack the requisite consciousness for female subjects (they are merely material objects). This example of a nineteenth-century pregnant wax mannequin (on the following page) is particularly distressing. The female model undergoes the birth of a child by cesarean section while her limbs are bound with white cloth. Details of the scene suggest a fantasized gang rape: the subject's body is incapacitated by her horizontal position and bindings. Her face registers pain and dismay, while her gaze is directed away from her body as if in a dissociative state. Her white (virginal) gown is cut to expose her vaginal and abdominal regions, which are probed by the disembodied hands of four men under the guise of extracting her child. Her body itself is cut open with a scalpel to extract the fetus buried within.[65] The religious and sexual signification of "ecstasy" this Anatomical Venus represents reminds us that cultural artifacts and feminine norms "are never truly neutral."[66]

Feminist Engagement with the Erotic Womb

Venus's enigmatic performance of woman as a desiring, agential, and feminine subject offers a positive reimagining of pregnant subjectivity. *How* the female body performs pregnancy shapes the agency and authority a woman enjoys. Mary's nonagential (submissive), nondesiring (asexual), feminine (relational) subjectivity signifies woman as mother and womb as sacred space. Athena's agential (assertive), nondesiring (asexual), and masculine (autonomous) pregnant subjectivity signifies woman as warrior and womb

La Césarienne, wax anatomical model, collection Spitzner, Université de Montpellier, France.

as political space. Venus's agential (assertive), desiring (sexual), and feminine (relational) subject signifies woman as lover and womb as erotic space. They mother, order, and harmonize the male world, respectively.

Pregnancy can grant a woman greater control over her life, allowing her to pursue her desires in an embodied way by navigating her womb—her embodied, creative potency—on her terms. Venus unites the feminine and masculine orders to resist the Mary-Athena binary. She also dissolves the normative division of motherhood into feminine and masculine modes of reproductivity and performs pregnancy as embodied desire *and* agency, a feminine expression of male power. Yet the objectifying force of male power, exercised on women's bodies through the male gaze, undermines sex's civilizing function by subjugating female beauty to male norms of desirability. The power of the male gaze and its erotizing force threaten to erase female agency entirely. Women's freedom from sexual dominance evaporates like Caelus's seafoam in the matrix of the male gaze.

Women need wombs of their own: opportunities to materialize embodied, (pro)creative intellectual and biological labor. But women must also transcend their wombs and materialize their subjectivity as part of an inviolable humanity. Appealing to the authority grounded in the material womb to correct or "mother" male associates and friends reinscribes woman with an inferior, bodily nature. Reductionistic norms and bodily performances of womanhood deprive women of robust subjectivity and moral authority. Wombed personhood remains a troubled concept.

We cannot reproduce Venus's subduing power over nature in today's world. Too much and too little have changed. Culture remains subject to, *rather than subjugating of,* nature because social and political systems privilege male power, experience, and desire. Indeed, the sexual coding of women and the eroticization of their bodily parts in contemporary constructions of heteronormative sexuality benefit men by reinforcing male power. Women who indulge their sexual desire risk sexual humiliation and degradation. Women who deny their sexual desire risk sexual impotency and dehumanization. Without the recognized capacity and freedom to decide when and with whom to act on their sexual desire, women are left with impossible choices—choices between sexuality and maternity (Mary) or maternity and power (Athena). The poles of chastity and promiscuity prove that for women, the personal is political.

Feminist readings of the pregnant subject must move beyond a resignification of sex alone to a cultural reimagination of female subjectivity: a refashioned vision of embodiment, a restored valuing of bodily work, a renewed veneration of feminine activities, and an ideology of reproduction that entails material and immaterial births.[67] Venus's performance of pregnant subjectivity as a desiring, agential, and feminine female subject provides a valuable template for women who have grown weary of the hegemony of the womb and long to actualize and experience wombs of their own making. Women desire to transcend the choice between feminine and masculine subject positions, between having children and having careers, and between child rearing and self-fulfillment. The question remains whether women can effectively transcend their metaphysical and material impoverishment and fulfill their pregnant potential in concrete ways.[68]

4

Playing Barbie

Womb as Material Space

I didn't want to be a Barbie doll. I didn't want to be a passive
entertainer. It wasn't how I wanted to present myself.
—Annie Lennox

Barbie is my role model. She might not do
anything, but she looks good doing it.
—Paris Hilton

The three-dimensional doll Barbie arouses considerable critical attention.[1] Ruth Handler, toy inventor and cofounder

of the Mattel Toy Company, created Barbara Millicent Roberts (Barbie) to overcome the functional limitations of paper dolls.[2] Barbie received a mixed reception when she debuted at the New York Toy Fair in 1959.[3] Today Barbie is the most popular fashion doll ever produced and the top fashion doll product in the United States.[4] More than one hundred Barbie dolls are sold every minute, which amounts to fifty-eight million dolls sold annually. A Barbie Dream House is purchased every two minutes. The Barbie YouTube channel is the top-rated YouTube brand among girls. Barbie enjoys 99 percent brand awareness globally. In 2020, Mattel's Barbie brand generated gross sales of 1.35 billion US dollars, up from 1.16 billion US dollars the year before. Barbie has shattered the toy ceiling, transcending her status as a child's doll. Barbara M. Roberts is a worldwide female icon.

Toys are designed to serve as props in children's games of make-believe.[5] Children imagine and play out creative scenarios as they manipulate artifactual objects like dolls, trucks, and blocks. They begin to believe in the logical possibilities of imagined events and actions: they begin to *make-believe.* Props coordinate their imaginative acts. Dolls, for example, enable children to represent and grapple with real-world social activities and relations. Because representational props like dolls are intentional props—they are intended to *count as* and *stand for* babies (or women in the case of Barbie)—they allow children to explore identity vicariously, practice roles they might someday assume, and investigate their feelings and perspectives.[6]

Barbie's successful facilitation of imaginative play helps explain her incredible market and cultural power.[7] When Handler created Barbie, she regarded the doll as a tangible sign of female choice: Barbie has more than two hundred occupations.[8] Barbie represents a fully grown woman with professional and personal dreams of her own—and a house, not merely a room, to go with them. She single-handedly wrests a future for herself without the support of a male figure, exemplifying her era's progressive call for women's independence from marriage and children. Barbie never marries Ken, her mostly steady companion, nor births Ken's children. Ken is simply her accessory.[9]

Unlike popular caricatures of feminists as angry, aggressive, man-hating women, Barbie represents female liberation in culturally appealing ways. Her physical perfection, concern for self-presentation, personal wealth, and professional achievements instantiate ideals that are largely commensurate with the American dream and its underlying material conception of success. She may operate like a fierce boss lady who prefers freedom, professional advancement, and economic privilege to a husband and kids, but Barbie also smiles, stays physically fit, maintains her good looks and elegant home, and dresses exquisitely. Her iconic projection of femininity conceals her tacit embrace of masculine values and removes the taint of feminism that undergirds her bodily identity. *Looking the part* of the ideal woman enables Barbie to pass as the ideal woman.[10]

But passing is as far as Barbie can go in a world that defines woman as womb. She does not bear children like

Mary and Venus, whose physical pregnancies align female subjectivity with bodily submission and labor. Nor does she engender civic order, like Athena, or spiritual discernment, like Venus, whose respective birthing of social goods associates female subjectivity with bodily redirection and sublimation. Barbie, rather, *projects but does not perform pregnant subjectivity.* She conveys a feminine signification but eludes feminine roles: she is husbandless and childless. Mattel deftly situates Barbie in occupations that serve others (medical doctor, teacher, friend) to define her as other directed. Barbie's service orientation stabilizes her female identity just enough to disarm buyers. Her unwombed yet feminine performance of subjectivity instantiates a new archetypal model of womanhood: *casting oneself as woman.*

To say that Barbie casts herself as a woman—that she *plays* woman by projecting pregnant subjectivity—is to say that she *suggests but never enacts pregnancy.* She codes woman as a reproductive subject, a human with a fertile womb, without performing pregnancy literally or figuratively. By standing for woman and exhibiting the feminine signs embedded in her wombed subjectivity, Barbie is able to refuse pregnancy while still affirming its feminine ground. Mattel pulls off this move by embedding Barbie in a matrix of female normativity that ties her trademark identity to domesticity (dream home) and bodily adornment (designer clothing). Signifying the motherless Barbie as ultrafeminine, in contrast to the motherless but masculine Athena, supplies the necessary condition for Barbie's material pregnancy even if her pregnancy, along with other female bodily activities, remains unrealized.

Mattel's positioning of Barbie for motherhood vis-à-vis femininity enables viewers to easily imagine her as a mother. Buyers are drawn to Barbie's normative representation of femininity in part because of its familiarity. Girls, for instance, participate in normalizing processes and disciplinary practices that affirm woman as mother and assign female value to domestic, bodily labor. Barbie's representation of woman as a contented, domestic creature stabilizes woman as womb: Barbie's feminine activities and identity signify fertility (we assume that feminine persons are reproducing persons). Barbie may never bear children, but her idealized representation of woman makes childbearing a logical outcome of her particular performativity. Because Barbie casts herself as a reproductive being, her lack of reproductivity does not transgress feminine norms—normative womanhood (femininity) requires only that woman *can and may* reproduce, not that she in fact *does* reproduce. Barbie's feminine identity validates her object status as a placeholder for woman. Her feminine identity also justifies the recursive projection of female activities from woman to doll (and vice versa), which allows Barbie to pass as an ideal woman. By situating Barbie within systems of female identity-making—and by projecting ideals of womanhood and material success onto Barbie—Mattel transforms cultural norms into consumer desires. Consumers can fulfill their desires by regarding Barbie as a prop or proxy for themselves. They can inhabit Barbie's world by purchasing Barbie and her accoutrements. And they can strive to embody Barbie, genuinely or subversively, as they play with concepts of womanhood embedded in Barbie's feminine form.

Barbie qua Mattel toy exercises agency through masculine norms. Like the constructed ideal man, she chooses career over caregiving and moves in and out of occupations without constraint or critique. In contrast to Athena, who is compelled into metaphoric motherhood to salvage her feminine identity, Barbie avoids both motherhood and the stigma of a masculine code by projecting an image of the ideal woman *without the supporting activities*, such as birthing babies, that authorize femininity. Her full breasts suggest but do not perform a nourishing function. Her vibrant smile implies youthful vitality despite her approaching senior status. Barbie's *casting of self as woman* disrupts prescriptive, normative constructions of womanhood. "Playing Barbie" plays us, while it is us who think we are playing with her.

Barbie's status as a toy frees her from the overtly performative conditions of femininity endured by Mary, Athena, and Venus. Yet her material nature—she is a toy sold for profit—destabilizes female identity in profitable ways. For instance, Mattel minimizes the masculinity that undergirds Barbie's subjectivity (as an unmarried, childless, professional woman) by feminizing her entire world. Pink houses, pink cars, and pink dresses encode Barbie as feminine (and therefore reproductive) despite her avoidance of marriage and motherhood. Her archetypal model of woman, encapsulated by the concept of womb as material (self-producing) space, arises from what she *casts* or *projects* materially, not from what she *does*.[11] Barbie exploits the material difference between feminine form (womb) and function (reproduction) to resist woman's bodily identity while securing her femininity. She thus transcends the womb, woman's legitimating source of authority and agency, *without* transcending the feminine body that contains it. Her imitation of ideal femininity fosters her iconic power.

True to her toy status, Barbie performs femininity not through bodily labor and reproduction but through the public projection of a female body *capable of* bodily labor and reproduction. Her projection of pregnant subjectivity negates the modern view that woman's essence or nature is bodily, that woman is an inherently reproductive creature, that woman is naturally situated in the domestic sphere, and that woman is properly assigned to the feminine order. Barbie transcends modernity's dualistic model of natural, binary sex and sex-based attributions through an endless, repetitious exercise of image construction and projection (self-production). She aptly materializes Judith Butler's injunction to work the trap of one's bodily confinement and labor.[12] Barbie's gender performativity resituates female subjectivity in culture rather than biological sex.[13] Her authenticating performance of woman—as a fashioned, groomed, shapely, successful, and *unwombed* female subject—problematizes the Cartesian mind-body construction of self. Further, her provocative independence from marriage and motherhood flouts the male-female construction of sex that treats woman as womb.[14]

Feminist interest in poststructural treatments of human nature and identity—as products of embedded structures—should be obvious. If gender is produced by discourse rather than biology, then gender categories (man and woman) bear different meanings in different contexts—that is, they are neither deterministic nor stable. If gender is a product of power rather than truth, if gender is bodily and nonverbal, if gender is expressed or performed through a stylized imitation or mimetic representation of gender conventions, then gender can be disrupted, exploited, subverted, and dissolved into a "convergence of gender identity" so that complex subject positions can emerge, positions that challenge the so-called fixed (and oppressive) content of the category "woman."[15]

Lest the feminist confetti be thrown prematurely and victory be declared over misogyny, there's a need to acknowledge important limitations of poststructural solutions to gender oppression. Poststructuralists contest materiality, such as the biological body, for the sake of disclosing conceptual and linguistic structures that give rise to women's limited agency. Judith Butler maintains in *Bodies That Matter* that although "materialities" of the body, signified by biological, anatomical, physiological, and hormonal claims, cannot be denied, the meaning of these materialities is conditioned, enabled, and limited by interpretative matrices.[16] She is undoubtedly right. And feminists must acknowledge and analyze the social processes that ascribe meaning to the female body, processes that Barbie and other representative examples and performances of woman expose as arbitrary and fluid. Yet feminists must also address the exigent materiality of women's embodied lives, as Beauvoir correctly observes. Human organisms, self-actualizing agents, have social *and* material value. By minimizing or ignoring the material dimensions of women's embodiment, by treating the reproductive womb as a cultural effect or source of oppression, we risk erasing women and their bodies altogether. It matters whether breasts signify spiritual nourishment or sexual desire. And it matters whether breasts are painful and diseased. Rich articulations of identity depend on complex accounts of gender that resist eliding embodiment.[17] Women are no more dolls than they are wombs.

We should also observe that performativity emerges in the confines of male power. Situating gender performativity within a lived matrix of diffuse social relations invites both implicit and explicit exercises of male power over and against gender construction and disruption. Handler's appropriation of male conceptions of beauty for Barbie indicates the troubling ways that dominant desires enter into women's psyches in insidious ways and shape, if not entirely construct, what it means to be (or perform) a woman.

Performativity enacts gender ideals that are produced and imposed through disciplinary practices (body shaming or body praising). Disciplining the female body to conform to (changing) conventions of womanhood is a material effect of male power. Think of Mary's modest dress, Athena's powerful arms, Venus's luxurious hair, and Barbie's minimal waist. These examples, along with dieting, waxing, tanning, and other exteriorized performances of "woman," exhibit embodied, stylized expressions of male desire. Subversion promises to disrupt conventional gender ideals and norms—parodic practices like drag expose the artificiality of gender performativity—but gender conformity does not disappear in a flash once we reveal its underlying operations. Indeed, performativity may inadvertently objectify women by appropriating female norms constructed through the lens of male control rather than autonomous, material, female concerns. Male preferences for specific kinds of female bodies may account for the changing averages of women's body weight over time. Within LGBTQIA+ cultures, butch presentations meant to challenge the conventions of femininity might also incite male fantasies of domination. Butler admits that gender performativity is not in and of itself an exercise in freedom. The "repetition of oppressive and painful gender norms" imprisons women in an exhausting, infinite cycle of imitation that fails to live up to constructed idealizations.[18] Acknowledging the linguistic and cultural dimensions of gender performativity does not neutralize the force of male hegemony on female subjects. Barbie exemplifies this fact perfectly.

Mattel's construction of female identity through the self-producing, representational work of Barbie simultaneously relaxes the biological rendering of woman as womb and intensifies the cultural rendering of woman as object. While Barbie decouples female identity from a biological system and the conventional reproductive activities they entail, her detachment fails to free her (and real women) from male control.

Avoiding marriage and children does not liberate women from psychic and bodily oppression. Even transcending mind-body dualism with its masculine-feminine markings does not safeguard women against oppressive structures of work and life. Nor does subverting gender through reiterative projections of pregnant subjectivity. Barbie may dominate the toy market—and, in her narrated history, succeed in a myriad of careers—but she very tangibly shows that female success in a man's world depends on male approval.[19]

Barbie as Mass-Produced Prop

Barbie is a plaything, a prop, in the child world of make-believe. She is an economic good, a consumer brand, and a human proxy in the adult world of image and profit.[20] While she represents woman generically in the fictive world of make-believe, she represents herself as a specific woman with a unique identity in the economy of marketed toys.[21]

Representational female dolls like Barbie have served historically as religious symbols and icons for ceremonial and educational purposes.[22] Today inanimate and animate female dolls tend to signify cultural views rather than distinctly spiritual or ethical values. Japan's popular Love Dolls, for instance—artificially intelligent humanoid silicone adult dolls that talk, sing, and yes, copulate—attract a market of men who repudiate relationships with real women but desire female companionship and sexual encounters.[23] One cannot roundly blame or shame them. Globally, marriage and monogamy have shed their originating ethical functions and theological meanings. Sexual desire has lost its mystical charge. Even Venus's seductive illustration of sexuality as a mechanism for transcendence from life's banality and a source of fecundity no longer exerts the same behavioral influence of earlier eras. Sex is less spiritual and literally more mechanical than ever. Yet the move from a sex doll to a sexualized person, typified by the projection of performative and normative expectations onto a female lover, is terrifyingly easy in the face of gender performativity and female objectification. Barbie is no Love Doll, but she is exploited by male desire all the same.[24]

Barbie qua woman is born ex nihilo from Handler's mind in the Mattel Toy Factory. She stands as a powerful symbol of female autonomy, Handler's and her own. She enters the world in the mold of Athena and Venus as a grown woman who requires no further maturation. Barbie negotiates the masculine order by appropriating Mary's virginity, Athena's power, and Venus's beauty for professional advancement and social acceptance. She mimics Athena's activity in the male world (and, like Athena, avoids mother-hood to do it). She embodies Venus's beautiful, seductive presence to minimize the threat of the masculine woman.[25] Barbie also bears an important kinship with Mary, the mother of Jesus: both are functional orphans. Barbie's vague past allows Mattel to design a world of professional and personal possibilities for her adult life just as Mary's little-known family history enables her readers to embrace biblical details of her miraculous encounters with divin-ity. In each case, the absence of ordinary family ties and constraints empowers Barbie and Mary to choose radical, extraordinary paths for themselves. Their narratives are rooted in adult relationships rather than family status. Their absence of personal responsibilities facilitates their authen-tic independence. Their untethered choices strengthen their autonomy.[26]

Barbie qua toy is manufactured and put into service by the Mattel Toy Company to increase the company's share of the toy market and profitability. She is the female face of a corporate entity that makes money she cannot enjoy, though Mattel grants Barbie qua woman substantial wealth of her own.[27] As a representational toy, a prop that stands for woman, Barbie mirrors the performative effects of Ameri-can femininity on female subjectivity: she is rich, admired, and beautiful by Euro-American standards. She also nor-malizes the modern material interface with reality through capital, a move that reinforces female objectification by treating woman as a cheap product for market exchange. Mary, Athena, and Venus enjoy cultural power because of their rich religious and social value; Barbie's cultural power rests upon Mattel's high profit margin. Barbie qua toy is an economic tool.

Mattel's appropriation of the female body for market exchange introduces an economic signification of female identity: *woman as commodity*. Packaging femininity for profit trivializes the experience of womanhood (as if being a woman is equivalent to being a manufactured, boxed up, supplied-upon-demand product). As with the case of Japan's Love Dolls, conveying normative womanhood through the medium of a toy eases the psychological move from woman toy (Barbie) to woman *as* toy (women as objects of utility). In fact, Barbie's global success pre-supposes the treatment of woman as an instrument for market exchange.[28] Mattel owns and exploits Barbie's model of womanhood for material gain. They package into her monetized dream life key elements of male fantasy: beauty, money, and freedom from spousal and child responsibility.

While Barbie as icon can embody a multiplicity of imagined and performed identities, Barbie as toy must be nothing. Mattel's success in the marketplace necessitates Barbie's reiterative erasure of identity. She must, during children's acts of play, vacate the identities Handler ascribes to her (medical doctor, astronaut, veterinarian) so that children can impose their constructed identities and life stories onto Barbie's physical form. The consumers' dreams and identities are primary in Barbie's service as a toy. She thus bears a functional similarity to Mary insofar as they both surrender their birth identities to operate as bodily vessels for another's desire.[29]

Mattel's instrumental use of femininity to sell Barbie's monetized world instantiates woman as a cheap commodity. Mattel explicitly markets Barbie's limitless capacity for manipulation as an ideal (even dreamy) marker of female subjectivity. Barbie is a pleasing, passive plaything. She can project vastly different identities when animated by a playmate, yet Barbie mirrors *and* markets the narrow strictures of her consumers' objectifying gazes. Her inscribed norms of femininity—her long hair, sparkling eyes, gleaming smile, and shapely figure—reflect man's surveilling judgment of attractiveness and desirability, exposing female vulnerability to power.[30]

Mattel's material concern for Barbie's function over her representational female form reflects the reductive nature of commodification in a mechanized world.[31] Competition for profit necessitates the mass production of commodified goods. Mass production leads to an expansion of goods on the market and an increase in market share. The proliferation of goods increases sales by lowering a product's individual cost per unit and enhancing a consumer's accessibility to the produced good. Profits rise as sales increase. Depersonalization is one of the more demoralizing cultural trade-offs of mass production. The exchange of commodified goods in a mechanized world necessitates sameness. Objects of mass production must necessarily look the same to appeal to a mass market of consumers who demand a particular good. Sameness is also a desirable feature among products designed for a specific purpose—for example, wagon wheels. This photograph of five unclothed Barbie dolls nicely illustrates depersonalization and also discloses a disjunction in the logic of verisimilitude underlying mass production. Human diversity defies a single or narrow set of object representations. But the pressures of mass production mandate that even representational objects violate the reality of human difference by mirroring nonrepresentational objects: Barbie dolls from different decades must look virtually identical. And as the process of objectification goes, so must real, living women.

Ponytail Barbie #4, 1960; Fashion Queen Barbie, 1963; Ash Blonde Bubble Cut Barbie, 1963; American Girl Barbie on Francie's body, 1965; and Sun Sensation Barbie, 1991. Private collection, photo by H. Wright.

Mattel profits by giving Barbie a shape that appeals cross-culturally. Efficiency goes up and costs go down when machines use a single or limited set of molds and materials on a production line. The absence of individuating physical (formal) features is both expected and desirable among commodified goods. Buyers expect exactness across individual units within brands. What an individual buyer does with his or her purchased product—the function or use of a canned food item, for example, in different recipes—facilitates an individualizing touch. Likewise, the projected individuality of particular Barbies—and, by extension, the uniqueness of the person for whom Barbie serves as a prop or proxy—is realized only by accessorizing the body and animating particular Barbie dolls through imaginative play. In short, Barbie is individuated through her function (enacted activities) rather than her form (physical parts). Individuality and uniqueness are therefore by-products rather than products of manufacturing. The nineteenth-century construction of self as a mechanized being within a system of manufactured goods generates both frightening and exhilarating implications for women.

On the one hand, defining woman by her womb, the norms her womb implies, and the experiences her womb entails treats women collectively as an unindividuated subset of bodily persons rather than rational, autonomous, individual subjects. Women are thus different from men but not different from one another. The historic positing of woman as logically *and* existentially equivalent—that is, situating female identity in a common, bodily (wombed) essence—alienates women from the nonbodily capacities of self that support agency and shape self-identity. The production of normative femininity through consumer goods limits women's self-defining and self-determining possibilities. On the other hand, as consumers appropriate Barbie's commodified femininity—as children use Barbie as a prop in games of make-believe and as adults deploy Barbie as a proxy for self—they reverse the manufacturing formula and detach female identity from Barbie's *function*. They sever, in other words, the normative ties between woman and reproduction. Barbie's *form* supports the separation of female subjectivity from the womb without transgressing feminine norms because Barbie's femininity is stabilized by her feminine form (by the projection of wombed personhood her physical form suggests). Specific roles, like wife and mother, are therefore not inherent to womanhood as Barbie performs it. Hence playing Barbie ironically (or parodically) subverts bodily constructions of female subjectivity. Barbie may just be a salvific figure after all.

Barbie as Artistic Medium

Barbie is the first thoroughly branded female archetype in modern history. The doll's iconic look has remained virtually unchanged since the late '50s. New skin tones and sizes have been added in recent years, but her facial features are remarkably the same. What has changed, however, is Barbie's cultural import. The Council of Fashion Designers of America, Inc. (CFDA) announced in May 2019 that Barbie would receive a major fashion award for the many times she inspired celebrity fashion choices.[32] Barbie's influence in human culture arises from her iconic power. She is deployed as a medium for cultural change and artistic expression. Her influence over social norms and practices gains purchase from the power of icons.[33]

Iconography is driven by a profusion of images that constitutes representation as reality.[34] Icons act as mirrors for society, mirrors that attract or repel individual viewers. Kylie Jenner—American media personality, founder and owner of the company Kylie Cosmetics, and daughter of Caitlyn Jenner and Kris Jenner—borrows the iconography of Barbie and the iconic package in which Barbie is sold for her 2018 Halloween costume. Jenner's self-fashioning as Barbie bears personal and professional significance. Jenner has built a makeup empire with a net worth of nine hundred million dollars in sales. Her appropriation of Barbie as

Kylie Jenner, "Life In Plastic, It's Fantastic"; Instagram

a costume signals an appreciation for—and an identification with—Barbie's model of female success. She replicates the Barbie color scheme and packaging perfectly, coding herself *as* Barbie rather than a person paying homage to Barbie. She embodies the image of Barbie qua doll, complete with the blonde wig and fabricated stand that holds Barbie in place inside the product box, to communicate her shared status with the global icon. Jenner is a prop, a proxy, in society's games of make-believe.

Jenner's presentation as Barbie also constitutes a marketing campaign. Barbie embodies womanhood ideally, an achievement real women fail to attain naturally but can approximate with the help of Kylie Cosmetics. Because performances of femininity entail an infinite cycle of imitation, Jenner, like Barbie, can bank on high product sales. Jenner's presentation of woman as doll (as opposed to a Mattel production of Barbie as Kylie Jenner) treats female identity as an effect of market forces and further alienates women from the lived experiences that give individual shape and meaning to female identity. Whether Jenner intends to identify with Barbie as a role model for female success (monied and beautiful) or appropriate Barbie to elevate her own global status (to displace Barbie), her embodiment of Barbie complicates feminine constructions of female subjectivity.

In contrast to Jenner's appropriation of Barbie, Beyoncé performs Barbie as cultural critique. Queen B's product package mirrors Mattel's original Black Barbie box from 1979, the first doll with "Afro-style hair."[35] Beyoncé adds the word *Black* above the cursive, trademark Barbie name just as Mattel had done in 1979, an add-on to the trademarked Barbie script that communicates what the company regards as its enduring value: (white) Barbie. Rather than style herself as the original Black Barbie, a Black imitation of Blackness, Beyoncé imitates white Barbie *but makes white Barbie Black*, subverting Mattel's implicit claim that whiteness is more valuable than Blackness. Her subversion turns on her embodiment of white Barbie. She wears the original Barbie's 1959 bathing suit rather than the 1979 Black Barbie's red and gold disco dress, and she imitates white Barbie's closed finger wave and rigid, nearly frozen, posture, a contestation of Black alienation from prescriptive norms of female embodiment that privilege whiteness. Beyoncé's performance exposes the pernicious cost of white power: you must sell yourself, your image, your body for profit.[36] Queen B may be sending a message to Jenner directly.

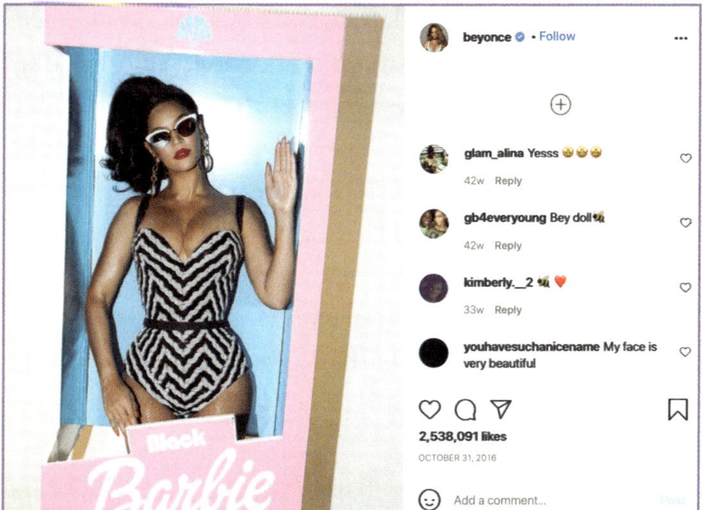

Beyoncé; Instagram

Trixie Mattel, winner of the 2018 RuPaul's Drag Race All Stars competition, extends the open performativity of Barbie to drag performance. Trixie adopts the Mattel name as her surname to solidify her performative embodiment of Barbie, a name that reinforces the manufactured nature of identities. Trixie rejects Barbie as her first name, however—a name that carries prescriptive, feminine baggage—and chooses instead Trixie, symbolizing woman as trickster (of men) or sex worker (turning tricks). Trixie's play with female sexuality challenges Barbie's assumed celibacy. Indeed, Trixie represents Barbie as a loud, self-deprecating, sexualized woman, a parody of the perfect, pure doll that disarms children and adults, and a manufactured imitation of woman produced through performative acts rather than codified sets of behaviors.[37] Trixie playfully exposes the artificiality of the Barbie dream world by removing Trixie (Barbie) from her box entirely.

Trixie also discloses Mattel's complicity in female alienation by reintroducing Barbie's origin story into her drag persona. Barbara, like Trixie, was born in Wisconsin. Barbara's transition to Barbie, symbolized by her geographical move from Wisconsin to California, parallels Trixie's own transition to the glamorous world of drag (the surfboard, ocean, and sand in this photo symbolize her new life in California and final transformation). Trixie's musical album is named Barbara, Barbie's given name, denoting the complexity of gender identity: one's birth identity may not be one's lived identity.

Mimetic disruptions of Barbie's dream world utilize the doll as a medium for cultural critique and subversion—to

Trixie Mattel; Twitter

comment on and subvert norms associated with Barbie. Trophy Wife Barbie (2016) is an Instagram photo series by the conceptual artist Annelies Hofmeyr.[38] The series features Barbie with antlers or stag horns, a masculine signification of woman, to represent woman as animal trophy, the label placed on Barbie as trophy wife.[39] The allusion to animal trophies serves to transform Barbie into an animal state and facilitates her engagement in "animalistic" activities—drinking, smoking, and the like. Hofmeyr's use of the materiality of the Barbie doll itself blurs the ontological boundaries between humans and dolls and calls into question the aptness of using children's toys to codify feminine norms and construct female identity. If Barbie were like real women and *actually* breastfed, drank, smoked, and so forth, female subjectivity might be, ironically, less bodily and much more cerebral.

"ArtActivistBarbie" seeks to disrupt female objectification by protesting female representation in art.[40] The Twitter feed series places Barbie next to museum and gallery paintings that feature women as artistic subjects in subordinate or objectifying positions. ArtActivistBarbie's purpose is to critique the hegemony of the art world. In this example, Barbie performs her original function of prop in a story to challenge the sexual objectification of women subjects in London's Wallace Collection. The real power of the series is that it gives Barbie a voice. No one speaks for her; rather, she instantiates her usual playful posture within a new role and persona: *art reporter and critic.* Barbie's self-referential play adds to the image's efficacy. She embodies objectifying beauty while critiquing female objectification.[41]

Annelies Hofmeyr (Trophy Wife Barbie), *Smoking Gun*, 2016.

Sarah Williamson, ArtActivistBarbie, *ArtActivistBarbie at the Wallace Collection*, "The Objectification of Women in the Wallace Collection Is Overwhelming! Every Where you Turn," 2020, photo by Sarah Williamson, academic art activist.

Feminist Engagement with the Material Womb

Barbie's dream world of mechanized mass production and consumerism commodifies womb as material space. Barbie challenges the production of femininity by locating the womb outside of the female subject entirely and decoupling womb from woman's identity. Her archetypal performance of female subjectivity situates femininity in form rather than function. Barbie projects femininity through mimetic images rather than bodily activity, enabling *playing* and *casting* and *passing* to serve as tools for gender disruption. Barbie situates the emergence of female subjects and their varied constructions of "pregnant" (self-producing) subjectivity within a context that is at least partly discursive. Barbie demonstrates how the production of different bodies yields different experiences of lived realities and identities. Barbie's archetype of woman expands female agency and identity beyond the interior womb to exterior expressions, including projections and performances, of self.

Viewed through the lens of postmodern pastiche, Barbie's body functions as a tool for gender critique and protest that exposes the oppressive structures of identity in creative, often parodic, ways. Barbie invites a new cultural imagining of pregnant subjectivity that challenges the subordinate, bodily construction of woman and transcends the mind-body (male-female) schema of self. Her *projected* performance of pregnant subjectivity—and celebrity appropriations thereof—authorizes her feminine attribution even though she lacks the sexual organs necessary for real pregnant subjectivity—namely, a vagina and uterus. "Woman's genitals are simply absent, masked, sewn back up inside their 'crack.'"[42] It is a good thing that Barbie's friend Midge is married and fertile.

Conclusion

The poet who never wrote a word and was buried at the crossroads still lives. She lives in you and in me, and in many other women who are not here tonight, for they are washing up the dishes and putting the children to bed. But she lives; for great poets do not die; they are continuing presences; they need only the opportunity to walk among us in the flesh. She would come if we worked for her, and that so to work, even in poverty and obscurity, is worthwhile.

—Virginia Woolf

Every speech should end *with a peroration. I find myself saying briefly and prosaically that it is much more important to be oneself* *than anything else.*[1] Deep in the female psyche resides the hard truth of what it means to live as a woman. Woman is vexed. She has a womb. To live, she must suffer in childbirth and relinquish her self-respect because being a woman is shameful.[2] She yearns for freedom and transcendence—*she longs to be herself*—still, she negotiates life as a subordinate, bodily subject, exacting freedom as she can without ever securing the authority to define herself in transhistorical terms. The message is clear: female identity is troubled by the womb.[3]

The bodily location of female identity is incontrovertible. Culture has figured the female sex as a womb: a person that gestates and bears children and thus produces and inhabits a feminine order. Woman's feminine signification distinguishes her from man. Laboring *as* (and with) a wombed body, managing the valences of pregnancy, conceals critical elements of self-identity directly accessible to man. Thinking, organizing, and acting are self-undertakings normalized as male. Woman's search for self, by contrast, starts with her wombed situation. How she negotiates her womb and the meaning of her reproductive labor can restrict or expand her freedom and ability to fashion a self on her terms. Woolf's injunction *to be oneself* unsettles woman.

While all human beings must negotiate the paradoxes of embodiment—men and women must both be and not be their bodies—walking around with a slowly distending abdomen makes the negotiation a public and ideological endeavor. Female bodies encode femininity into their performances of woman. Female bodies that lack wombs perform womanhood by inhabiting feminine spaces and performing feminine labor, such as caregiving and cooking. Just as wombs and woman signify one another, femininity and fertility imply one another. Femininity thus stabilizes the signification of woman as womb. The logic of female subjectivity—the intermingling concepts of *woman as womb, womb as feminine space*, and *femininity as the stabilizing force of female identity*—unravels as woman reconceives her womb as a source and site of liberation. Treating the womb as self-producing—as birthing one's ideas and activities—destabilizes the wombed construction of womanhood. *Women are their bodies in a way that men are not.* But this truth is not good feminist gospel.

Resistance to essentialist constructions of woman is integral to feminist thought. Powerful indictments of women's complicity in female objectification move women to question their performances of woman and the bodily identity their performances produce. Although I have not outgrown Beauvoir's deep-seated ambivalence about pregnancy and maternity, I seek to contest the wombed construction of woman, revalue wombed labor, and reintegrate wombed bodies into women's experience of self.

This book challenges readings of the womb that limit women's agency and self-understanding. Because women cannot avoid their wombs—real or projected; empty or impregnated—they would do well to reimagine pregnancy as a self-constituting and self-affirming phenomenon rather than a biological event, a public and private affair, literally and figuratively conceived, that contracts and expands women's sense of self. As a woman, mother, philosopher, and feminist, I have learned to navigate the ambiguity of pregnant subjectivity, of both being and not being my wombed body. Constructing identity when one lives with (as) a womb also means constructing an identity in relation to a real or hypothetical other—a fetus growing in the womb, a potential partner who could help create the fetus, a potential future fetus, and other unfolding relationalities.

"Woman" in this book is a discursive and iconographic subject, a narrative sign of womanhood. Configuring woman narratively and calling out her iconographic modes and meanings discloses how historic archetypes of womanhood shape contemporary female identity and experience. Narrative constructions of woman also recognize as "woman" persons who identify as women but lack uteruses. Normatively feminine bodies emerge in ideological constructions of the womb. But such bodies are not essential to the concept of "woman."

Resolving the Womb

There is no single truth of what it means to live as a woman. Rather, there are multiple expressions of lived experience born of our complex heritage that encompass the very different archetypes of woman analyzed in this book. *Athena to Barbie* demonstrates four ways that women have sought to solve their vexed, bodily nature. Mary, the young Jewish mother of Jesus, codifies the concept of woman as vessel, a literal and figurative container for the creation and sustenance of others. Her signification of womb as sacred space and representation of woman as mother exerts a powerful, pervasive influence on ideologies of the feminine subject. D'Agoty exaggerates the divine associations between Mary and motherhood in this mezzotint of female corpses and fetuses to attribute sanctity to reproduction and eradicate the possibility of sexual transgression. The coding of womb as sacred provides some liberatory potential for women by elevating their status within the masculine order. Marking the wombed body as sacred, however, diminishes the self-directing dimension of embodiment

Jacques Fabien Gautier d'Agoty, Two anatomical paintings: *left*, a pregnant female dissected figure, lateral view, with arms upraised; *right*, a seated female dissected figure holding a dissected baby (1773). Courtesy of the Wellcome Library, London, England.

that undergirds first-person understandings of self. Arguably, the Marian concepts of *woman as womb* and *woman as pure* dominate contemporary performances of womanhood. All women, mothers and nonmothers, must contend with the Marian ideology of womanhood.

Athena, the "woman-goddess" of Greek mythology, signifies womb as political space. Athena's model of motherhood and the epistemic advancement she symbolizes come with a twist: she's celibate. She, more than all the

Rudolph Tegner, *Pallas Athene*, 1921–22, Rudolph Tegner Museum, Dronningmølle, Denmark.

other archetypes of the pregnant subject, represents the exclusion of the feminine from the masculine world: *women birth bodies* (a feminine task) or *women birth ideas* (a masculine task) but not both. Athena's unwombed performance of woman remains a pernicious part of the Western psyche and civic order. Even if the average woman never invokes Athena by name or identifies her as an explicit ideal of womanhood, she knows intimately the reality Athena introduces into the Western world: femininity is a bodily performance, and reproduction is its central act. Since women's "real" power originates in their wombs, Athena's lack of fertility intensifies, rather than eases, the female burden. Athena crystallizes how biological reproduction authorizes women's economic activities and political rights, including the right to "mother" male politicians, coworkers, and colleagues by condemning or correcting their misbehavior.

Venus—the Roman goddess of love, sex, beauty, and fertility—is, like Mary, associated with sexual propriety. Venus also aligns archetypally with Athena by giving birth to the state: she is the mother of Aeneas, the founder of Rome. She facilitates a decidedly erotic turn in women's search for self. A once-prominent subject of artworks, Venus's identity is appropriated for medical school mannequins and dolls, figures that are styled, dressed, touched, cut, and displayed, as exemplified by this 1782 Clemente Susini life-size dissectible Venerina (little Venus). Venus is further transformed in the growing culture of the spectacle—from a mythological subject, art object, and teaching tool to a titillating doll

Clemente Susini, *Venerina* (Little Venus), life-sized dissectible wax model, 1782. Courtesy of Museo di Palazzo Poggi— Università di Bologna, Italy.

with her organs (and fetus) on display. The introduction of sexual allure into wombed identity transforms the ecstasy of reproduction "from a religious, mystical experience to an erotic one."[4] The pregnant subject becomes a passive object for cultural consumption rather than an active subject for analysis or an autonomous, authoritative figure. Venus is a challenging archetype for women because of her associative reduction of the feminine order to sexual operations. This is a regrettable reduction of her harmonizing work: she treats sex and procreation as dually sacred (Marian) *and* civilizing (Athenian) activities.

The packaged beauty of Barbie instantiates woman as commodity. Barbie drives an economy built upon the treatment of woman as an instrument for economic exchange and manipulation. She sells an idea of female perfection buyers can possess and embody with the aid of personal capital. Barbie not only facilitates the modern, monetary interface with reality; she also transforms the female body into a cheap consumer good. Barbie births female commodification, introducing into contemporary culture the concept of woman as a site and source of consumer desire. She signifies womb, the figurative space for female subjectivity, as material space.

The transference of material (corporeal and economic) desire onto Barbie bears upon pregnant subjectivity in uncanny ways. On the one hand, Barbie invites children and grown-ups alike to evaluate women's bodies, including pregnant bodies, for normative successes and failures. Mattel has yet to produce a pregnant Barbie—Barbie and

Midge & Baby—Happy Family, 2002, private collection, photo by H. Wright.

Ken never married, so a pregnant Barbie would transgress market norms. But Barbie's pregnant friend Midge, who is married to Alan and with whom she shares a three-year-old son, Ryan, is available for purchase. Midge's baby bump and the female fetus inside it (the box tells us she is having a girl) can be removed or added without altering her perfect proportions, as shown here. As the contemporary cult of the baby bump grows, so does the market for idealized postbaby bodies, ones that look exactly as they did before pregnancy, as if pregnancy were just a bump in the road of female normalcy. On the other hand, the artificiality of Barbie's packaged femininity exposes the absurdity of woman as commodity. The contemporary critique of woman as a material object aligns well with the disclosure of gender as a construct of language and power, including market power. Barbie has become a powerful tool among artists, celebrities, and drag performers for contesting and subverting female identity, white hegemony, and gender normativity.

Barbie performs femininity both as a modern exemplar of womanhood and as a postmodern critic of commodified subjectivity. She is, unlike Mary, Athena, and Venus, an actual prop and proxy in diverse *and* disruptive games of make-believe. Her enigmatic signification of womb as material space offers a dually constraining and liberating conception of womb as a site and source of consumer goods and constructed identities. Womb as material space challenges feminists to reforge bodily norms in the construction of female subjectivity.

Reading Woman

Mary's submissive, asexual, relational archetype of womanhood signifies woman as mother. Mary performs pregnancy as an untainted vessel who bears a sacred obligation to discharge God's call to reproduce the human world. She signifies womb as sacred space. Athena is an assertive, asexual, independent pregnant subject. She signifies woman as warrior and womb as political space. Athena performs pregnancy as a wise leader who suspends her feminine functions to enter into the masculine order. Venus is an assertive, sexual, relational pregnant subject. She signifies woman as lover and womb as erotic space. Venus performs pregnancy as an alluring goddess who uses her sex appeal to sublimate male aggression, subdue psychic angst, and unite men and women through physical intimacy and reproduction. Unlike Mary, Athena, and Venus, Barbie neither bears children, engenders civic order, nor facilitates spiritual discernment. Barbie, rather, *projects but does not perform pregnant subjectivity.* She conveys a feminine signification—she is an assertive, asexual, relational female icon—while eluding feminine roles. Her unwombed yet feminine performance of female subjectivity instantiates a new archetypal model of womanhood: *casting oneself as woman.*

Mary delivers, Athena conquers, Venus subdues, and *Barbie plays* the masculine order. They mother, organize, harmonize, and subvert the male world, respectively, through their archetypal performances of womanhood. Although these archetypes of woman do not resolve the centrality of the womb for female identity, each typifies the lived reality of the female subject. Together, they encapsulate the sources of wombed identity and the meaning of womanhood that women navigate even today. Their shared value lies in their illustrative movement from woman as sacred vessel to consumer good, a movement from submission to subversion.

Venus's popular appeal shows that growing numbers of women are unwilling to suspend feminine exercises of power for the sake of social stability. Intimacy, relationality, physical pleasure, love, ecstasy, transcendence, children, political engagement, civic leadership, professional choice, recognition, and equality—women want to experience these social goods like Venus: as desiring, agential subjects. Venus's harmonizing work extends to reproductivity itself: she treats sex and procreation as dually sacred (Marian) *and* civilizing (Athenian) activities. By inscribing pregnancy with religious and political meaning, Venus effectively marries Mary's feminine and Athena's masculine performances of subjectivity. Similarly, her signification of womb as erotic space powerfully unites women and men in the shared project of childbirth and suggests a more equitable distribution of power around childcare roles. Venus's unification of feminine and masculine signs also frees couples to reimagine their embodied performances of subjectivity by challenging the gender breakdown and coding of parental activities and perhaps progresses further by enabling an appreciation for nonbinary and transgender positionalities.[5] Mary and Athena's perceived surrender of female agency and feminine power irritates women who want to bring about a Woolfian state of affairs: securing equitable educational, economic, and cultural resources for men and women along with comparable freedoms of thought, time, and space.

Each archetype of woman is wanting. There are no permanent or fixed pathways to female agency and identity. But—*and here is the good feminist news*—there is a promise, a hope, a heuristic move embedded in these icons. Mary discloses the body's spiritual force. Athena gives birth to ideas. Venus saves intimacy from its cultural impoverishment. And Barbie subverts the womb in culturally appealing ways. While the pregnant subject is not identical with her body, the lived experience of pregnancy complicates her self-understanding.

This book is a feminist call to reconstitute the meaning and role of pregnancy in women's search for self. I ask that we refuse to read pregnancy as women's capitulation to patriarchy and instead treat pregnancy as an inherently ambiguous phenomenon: a liminal event and liminoid experience (and, yes, a public and private affair). This means we will acknowledge that pregnancy performs the important function of preserving the human species and, in the process, constrains female bodies by way of medical, psychological, cultural, aesthetic, and other external forces. We will also notice and affirm how female bodies exceed these controlling forces and render normative practices absurd that women can or will no longer perform.

We must contest what it means to live with a womb so that we are prepared to resist and persist in a world ungrateful for women's role in human reproductivity. We are beneficiaries of resistors who came before us; we are obliged to enrich the process of becoming a woman for our sisters yet to come.

We must affirm and move beyond Beauvoir's conceptualization of women as a collective, generic essence (womb) and identity (Other). Moving *beyond but with* Beauvoir involves examining a range of archetypal female subjects who represent distinct significations of womb: sacred, political, erotic, and material.

We must look anew at the concrete world of diverse women, a world in which female essence and identity are highly contested. Trans women without wombs, married lesbian women with biological children, married straight women without children, women who birth children through surrogates or with the aid of assisted reproductive technology (ART): the diversity of persons who identify as female is substantially greater than ever before. Yet the essential bind between "woman" and her womb—the embodiment of femininity through material performativity, particularly pregnancy—remains relatively fixed.

We must reassess the philosophical commitments that underlie and drive female identity in a postmodern direction. Poststructuralists exploit the gaps (slippages) between signifiers (Barbie, for example) and the signified (woman), gaps that allow individuals to successfully *express* or perform an identity without assuming historic meanings or conditions entirely. Trans women, for instance, may perform femininity without bodily reproductivity. Yet they are viewed suspiciously because they have not birthed children and do not code "properly" as women. *Who* woman is may be fluid, but *what* woman is remains stubbornly static.

We must challenge the biological signification of woman's womb so that she may birth nonmaterial children—books, political strategies, vaccines, and the like—and expand female sources of self-identity beyond bodily practices and norms.

We must contest the negative valuation of bodily labor and the physical laborers who perform it (disproportionately ethnic, racial, and gender minorities) and authorize men to engage in wombed labor. Straight, cisgender fathers can perform "motherly" childcare duties without fearing a loss of male authority if these duties no longer hold a female signification—that is, if soothing, feeding, and nurturing children is not a female-exclusive or feminine-coded activity. Similarly, transgender parents can care for their children without compromising their gender identities if childcare duties lose their gendered (male and female) significations. In this way, heterosexual, cisgender men can come to appreciate the plight of transgender parents.

The Woolfian task, *to be oneself,* is also the task of this book. Women will (and must) go on having babies, and they will also create new, liberating pathways for individual self-making. *Women must have money and a room of their own (and fewer children)* on Woolf's account to conceive and birth original, authentically expressed ideas.[6]

Women must have standing over the body's real and metaphoric productivity, sexual and asexual in nature. We should be valued for the labor we perform. We should have license to equitably engage and shape the world in which we find ourselves. We should be free to explore, realize, appreciate, and signify pregnancy in literal and figurative ways—by having children *or not having* children—without social contempt, projected deviance, loss of authority, or masculinizing affect. We should be willing to reassess femininity in light of consumer forces. We should experience the encouragement that is so generously and abundantly offered to men "to put on the body they have so often laid down" and give birth to themselves.[7] We should develop and appropriate diverse female archetypes—models like Mary, Athena, Venus, Barbie, and more—that incite us to reimagine ourselves in relation to disciplines of womanhood, diverse female communities, and deeply generative activities. We should, to channel Beauvoir, be capable of transcending our immanent, bodily states (and duties like cleaning, cooking, and caregiving) to pursue meaningful, emotionally fulfilling projects even if these projects begin with a struggle for freedom. And we should fulfill the obligations that follow from our liberation: to challenge oppressive models of female subjectivity, to resist female objectification, to affirm and embody diverse performances of pregnancy—*beyond* Mary, Athena, Venus, and Barbie—and, for more than a moment, disrupt female subordination by demanding rooms of our own.

Notes

Introduction

1 These opening lines are an intentional, improvised appropriation of the opening of Virginia Woolf's *A Room of One's Own*. Woolf's essay serves as a pervasive rhetorical partner in my analysis of pregnant subjectivity and the inspiration for the book's thesis and title. See Virginia Woolf, *A Room of One's Own* (New York: Harcourt, Brace, 1929).

2 Woolf, 4.

3 The term *pregnable* reveals much about the subjectivity of women. The idea of being assailed or vulnerable to attack maps onto the understanding of pregnancy (sperm attacking and penetrating the egg) as well as the concept of woman as weak and in need of male protection.

4 Woolf writes, "Here then was I (call me Mary Beton, Mary Seton, Mary Carmichael, or by any name you please—it is not a matter of

any importance)" (*Room of One's Own*, 6). From the Scottish ballad of Mary Hamilton:

> *Yestreen the Queen [Mary, queen of Scots] had four Maries,*
> *The nicht she'll hae but three.*
> *There was Mary Seaton an Mary Beaton,*
> *an Mary Carmichael an me.*

See "The Queen's Four Maries," Scots Language Centre, Centre for the Scots Leid, accessed August 18, 2020, https://www .scotslanguage.com/articles/node/id/436.

5 Woolf, *Room of One's Own*, 6.
6 Woolf, 199.
7 Woolf, 197.
8 I include this improvised line from William Shakespeare's *Hamlet* (to be or not to be) to evoke Simone de Beauvoir and the central idea that motivates *The Second Sex*: one is not born but becomes a woman. Woolf suggests a similar concept when she describes the process of altering one's embodied situation for the sake of creative freedom. Simone de Beauvoir, *The Second Sex*, trans. Constance Borde and Shiela Malovany-Chevallier (London: Jonathan Cape, 2009)

Chapter 1

1 Elizabeth A. Johnson, "The Mighty from Their Thrones," in *Advancing Mariology: The Theotokos Lectures 2008–2017*, ed. Jame Schaefer (Milwaukee, WI: Marquette University Press, 2017), 237. Johnson writes powerfully about Mary's wombed activity and associations from a Roman Catholic feminist theological perspective. Johnson retired from Fordham University in 2018 but not from feminist theology, I am delighted to say.
2 Concepts of woman as *object*, *opening*, and *Other* emerge, respectively, in the work of Mary Wollstonecraft, *A Vindication of the Rights of Woman: With Strictures on Political and Moral Subjects*, ed. D. L. Macdonald and Kathleen Scherf (Peterborough, ON: Broadview, 1997); Andrea Dworkin, *Intercourse*, 20th anniversary ed. (New York: Basic Books, 2007); and Simone de Beauvoir, *The Second Sex*, trans. Constance Borde and Sheila Malovany-Chevallier (London: Jonathan Cape, 2009). I continue to mine

these texts for their rich phenomenological insights and apt pain points. Female alterity continues to authorize women's subordinate position—woman as object of beauty for male pleasure, woman as reproductive animal, and so on—and undermine female equality. With the current rise in regressive politics, there is no more imperative time than now to challenge female objectification.

3 The feminist imagination thwarts the idea of wombs as essential or primary sources of women's authentic fruitfulness ("blessed is the fruit of your womb"). What it means for women to live fruitfully remains an open question and is not, from my perspective, a question that implies reproductive labor or bodily labor strictly understood. "Fruitfulness" should encompass intellectual and emotional labor so that women's activity in the world is equally valued, recognized, and integrated into civic and social structures.

4 I read Mary through the lenses of feminism and confessionalism. While my feminist views largely reflect second-wave presuppositions, I affirm—and am making gestures toward—contemporary feminist claims that challenge second-wave ideas like a sex-gender distinction. I am especially indebted to feminists who adopt phenomenological readings of the material, corporeal body (empirical realities of the female body matter a great deal in debates about women's agency and authority), women like Helen Marshall and Elizabeth Grosz. My theism is deeply Protestant with a high regard for Mary. My late mother-in-law, who painted the female figure on the book cover, was Roman Catholic. She shaped my views of Mary. Donna Griffith, however, a member of my childhood church, planted the seeds of my dual feminist-confessionist reading of Mary. Donna organized a church group for girls called "The M&M Club," which stood for "The Mary and Martha Club" (a different Mary). The M&M Club, which I joined when I was eight, studied women in the Bible, a remarkable feat given the exclusion of women in our church from preaching, serving as elders or deacons, and administering the sacraments of baptism and communion. My interest in women's studies took root in that club and later developed into an academic interest in feminist philosophy under the guidance of Carolyn Korsmeyer. My faith and Christian perspective have developed too. I am a member of First Presbyterian Church of Waco, Texas, a church with a majority female staff led by a gifted woman senior pastor, the Reverend Doctor Leslie

King. I regard Mary as a real historical figure who birthed Jesus, son of God, *and* a figure who has been subjected to sexist cultural readings that normalize narrow, bodily views of womanhood.

5 Conceiving womb as self-producing—that is, not merely as a material organ for biological reproduction but also as a semiotic organ for creative productivity—liberates the female psyche from the bodily constraints of femininity. Reading womb as a source and sign of female productivity also nicely expands the potential archetyping of the female subject beyond reproductive roles. Significations of woman inform but do not fix women's identities and experiences because gender is a fluid phenomenon. Women may understand who and what they are in light of accrued definitions and embedded social experiences, but they may also re-create and reproduce themselves by challenging and transcending past paradigms through their unique, creative endeavors.

6 I want to acknowledge that some female bodies do not have a womb (trans women) and some male bodies do have a womb (trans men).

7 Conceiving of wombs as sacred spaces motivates the conservative, evangelical Christian rejection of civil unions and same-sex marriages. Following the conservative logic, pregnancy loses its divinity outside of heterosexual marriage because the conditions for sanctification are unmet. Unmarried mothers, trans mothers, and assisted reproductive technology (ART–assisted mothers) all subvert womb as sacred space.

8 Dorian Llywelyn, "Mirror of Justice, Mother of Mercy," in Schaefer, *Advancing Mariology*, 290.

9 Although pregnancy and motherhood, normative performances of femininity, authorize women's agential status, women who forego pregnancy and motherhood do not lack agency and authority entirely. In fact, they may enjoy high degrees of agency and authority through appropriations of male subjectivity. Athena (chapter 2) is an archetypal example. Women's unwombed performances of female subjectivity, however, mark woman as masculine, a threat to the male world's reliance on gender normativity. Complete subversions of male power necessitate a deconstruction of femininity and masculinity.

10 Jane Schaberg examines the historicity and transmission of Jesus's illegitimacy in her powerful and aptly named book *The Illegitimacy*

of Jesus: A Feminist Theological Interpretation of the Infancy Narratives (San Francisco: Harper & Row, 1987). Her examination takes up the legacy of purity and sanctity that Mariology typically creates for women, which she regards as a tool for "institutional sexism" (12). Schaberg believes the truth behind Jesus's conception is likely a violent one, observing that "rape as well as seduction or adultery would be a normal way of accounting for Mary's pregnancy" (19). Schaberg claims further that the New Testament infancy narratives transmit the tradition of Mary's seduction or rape in the pregospel period, and moreover, his illegitimacy had a positive theological and christological (or christotypical) interpretation (163). Fear of association with sin and fornication has pushed against this reading, as has sexism (198). I have, like others before me (including Rosemary Radford Ruether, whom Schaberg names), attempted to reimagine Mary as a source of authentic, feminine creativity. I hope this reimagination will continue. But writing today, I land where Schaberg lands, which is to say that Mary is not a free and undefeated subject with her own inviolate agency and authority; rather, Mary represents a theology of repressed female subjectivity, a theology that is "unacceptable in its sexism, scapegoating female sexuality for sin and death" (198).

11 Beverly Roberts Gaventa, *Mary: Glimpses of the Mother of Jesus* (Columbia: University of South Carolina Press, 1995), 46. Gaventa and Rachel Fulton Brown give important weight to the stories of Mary's childhood in the temple. Gaventa devotes particular attention to the social and psychological role of these stories in shaping Mary's image and power (2), whereas Brown maintains that the stories enabled early Christians to show how Mary fulfilled scriptural narratives. Rachel Fulton Brown, "Mary in the Scriptures," in Schaefer, *Advancing Mariology*, 228–29.

12 Brown, "Mary in the Scriptures," 208.

13 Gaventa, *Mary: Glimpses*, 46. I intentionally play with the idea of an "expectant" mother and coin the term "unexpectant" rather than "unsuspecting" mother to describe Mary because of her cognitive relationship with the divine. She does not initially desire or expect to be pregnant prior to her marriage. Thus "surprise" does not adequately capture her cognitive state when she learns that she will be impregnated by the Holy Spirit. Her pregnancy news is unexpected news.

14 Gaventa, 66, 72–73.

15 Jaroslav Pelikan, David Flusser, and Justin Lang, *Mary: Images of the Mother of Jesus in Jewish and Christian Perspective* (Minneapolis: Fortress Press, 2005), 8.

16 Gaventa, *Mary: Glimpses*, 86; and Luigi Gambero, *Mary and the Fathers of the Church: The Blessed Virgin Mary in Patristic Thought*, trans. Thomas Buffer (San Francisco: Ignatius, 1999), 46.

17 Contrary to most contemporary biblical scholars, Rachel Fulton Brown makes a compelling case that Mary is indeed quite prominent in Scripture. Brown traces premodern representations and descriptions of Mary to ancient temple worship and textual analysis. She finds exegetical legitimacy, supported by the work with ancient texts by Margaret Barker, that Mary is everywhere in the Old Testament in the figure of the Lady as Mother of the Lord (Brown, "Mary in the Scriptures," 210). This figure was once prominent in older temple worship—older than the Law of Deuteronomy—and later rejected as part of the reforms of King Josiah and postcaptivity Israelites. Brown maintains that Barker's reading of ancient texts reproduces the readings of Scriptures found in later medieval and early modern tradition. For her part, Barker claims that "without the Lady, without the Mother, there would be no Christianity because it was the Lady who made the LORD, quite literally, by anointing him" (229). Barker has devoted seventeen books thus far to developing her reading of the "temple tradition" (230).

18 Brown, 225–26.

19 Brown, 221.

20 Gaventa notes in the foreword to *Mary: Glimpses* that the Marian Library at the University of Dayton exceeds eighty-five thousand books and pamphlets (2). Elizabeth Johnson outlines the numerous artifacts—paintings, poetry, hospitals, and more—associated with Mary (Johnson, "Mighty," 237). Brown also comments on Mary's various identities and associations (Brown, "Mary in the Scriptures," 220–21).

21 Gaventa, *Mary: Glimpses*, 15.

22 Gaventa acknowledges that Christian theologians debate the meaning and temporal bounds of Mary's virginity. Orthodox theologians, for example, reject the doctrine of the Immaculate Conception (15), yet the Protoevangelium of James obsesses over Mary's "sacred purity" (109–10).

23 The Protoevangelium of James is especially important here. A woman checks Mary's vaginal vault to see whether she is a biological virgin. Her hand catches fire. David Flusser describes Mary as "an ideal [woman] for generations of women." Once she was elevated to holiness, Flusser argues, "Mary became for the believing Christian a paradigm and exemplar of what Christians could become. The more Mary was understood to be human, the more she became a model for them. The belief in her virginity need not lead to an unnatural asceticism but can protect the believer from unchasteness and lead toward a spotless and shining purity" (Pelikan, Flusser, and Lang, *Mary: Images*, 10).

24 Evangelicalism has long espoused sexual abstinence before marriage, so much so that evangelicals have generally presupposed and encouraged marriage. Roman Catholics have celebrated lifelong singleness and abstinence—and exerted less pressure to marry—in a way that is rarely seen among Protestants. I thank Andrew Arterbury and Douglas Weaver for clarifying the Roman Catholic and evangelical stances on marriage and sexual practices.

25 As I explain in the previous note, conservative Christians believe sexual intimacy is reserved for marriage (and, since the 2015 affirmation of marriage equality in *Obergefell v. Hodges*, have defined marriage as exclusively heterosexual). Some of the Christian resistance to same-sex marriage and intimacy has pointed to same-sex couples' inability to reproduce children and, thus, a thwarting of the biblical exhortation in Genesis 1:28 to "be fruitful and multiply."

   With the advent of assisted reproductive technologies (ART) and the mitigation of reproductive barriers, the conservative argument now specifies "natural" (bodily) conception and reproduction. Evangelical resistance to ART faces some difficulty, then, in embracing Mary, who is regarded (at least in the Roman Catholic tradition) as someone who was impregnated by the Holy Spirit and who herself was immaculately conceived.

26 Gambero, *Mary and the Fathers*, 54. Gambero characterizes Eve as a ruined, though virginal, woman whose disobedience ruins the human race because it "imposed the bonds of spiritual slavery" (54) upon human beings.

27 I do not hold this view, but I appreciate its appeal given the stigma of female sexuality and the trauma generated by sexual violence.

28 Grace does not cover all sins, it seems.

29 "Grant me chastity and continence," prays Saint Augustine of Hippo, "but not yet." Augustine, *Confessions*, trans. Henry Chadwick (Oxford: Oxford University Press, 1998), bk. 8, p. 145.

30 Margaret D. Kamitsuka challenges the pro-life narrative of evangelical Christian culture and its interpretation of the biblical text. She claims that the Bible says little on the issue of abortion and that the early church fathers, on whom evangelical and conservative Roman Catholics rely, have complicated views of abortion and certainly offer no blanket condemnations thereof. Margaret D. Kamitsuka, *Abortion and the Christian Tradition: A Pro-Choice Theological Ethic* (Louisville, KY: Westminster John Knox, 2019).

31 Helen Marshall describes the phenomenological fluidity of pregnancy in "Our Bodies, Ourselves: Why We Should Add Old Fashioned Empirical Phenomenology to the New Theories of the Body," in *Feminist Theory and the Body: A Reader*, ed. Janet Price and Margrit Shildrick (New York: Routledge, 2010), 64–75. Marshall maintains that the experience of pregnancy is not, as we might believe, a unified experience; rather, it is more like a self "living in the usual fragmented way, with pregnancy as one of the fragments" (67). She includes in her essay several journal entries she composed during her pregnancy, entries that capture a fluctuating sense of self formed and reformed in response to medical literature, other women's experiences of pregnancy, and her own unpredictable physiological changes, described as "shifts rather than a simple progression of growth in size" (73).

32 Francesca Aran Murphy, "Mary as 'Omnipotent by Grace,'" in Schaefer, *Advancing Mariology*, 200.

33 Murphy, 200.

34 Murphy, 201.

35 Murphy, 198.

36 I am grateful to Andrew Arterbury for sharing his expertise on the biblical presentation and subsequent commentaries on Mary. Very little is said about Mary in either location. Luke 1:35–50 highlights Mary's consent to God's will, but the primary emphasis is on the Spirit's work. Mary looks like a faithful disciple.

37 Jaroslav Pelikan, *Mary through the Centuries: Her Place in the History of Culture* (New Haven, CT: Yale University Press, 1996), 41.

38 Article XVIII of the Southern Baptist Convention's 2000 "Baptist Faith and Message" is devoted to the family and describes the

husband-wife relationship as, respectively, a relationship of love and submission. Southern Baptist Convention, "The Baptist Faith and Message," September 1, 2016, https://tinyurl.com/mfpu6bsw.

39 Pelikan, *Mary through the Centuries*, 42–43.

40 Sandra Lee Bartky, "Foucault, Femininity, and the Modernization of Patriarchal Power," in *Feminist Theory Reader: Local and Global Perspectives*, 4th ed., ed. Carole R. McCann and Seung-Kyung Kim (New York: Routledge, 2017), 466–80. Bartky aptly articulates the idea of a *produced* feminine body-subject, a production generated through normative, disciplinary practices like hair care, makeup, and so forth: "The disciplinary practices I have described are part of the process by which the ideal body of femininity—and hence the feminine body-subject—is constructed; in doing this, they produce a 'practiced and subjected' body, that is, a body on which an inferior status has been inscribed" (472). I extend her analysis to include maternity as a cluster of disciplinary practices that produce the ideal feminine body-subject, the pregnant subject. Susan Bordo also draws on the work of Michel Foucault in her powerful analyses of the female (and male) body. Her analyses, like Bartky's, have certainly shaped my thinking about the pregnant subject, and I am grateful for their advancement of feminism in an era unfriendly to feminists. See, for example, Susan Bordo, "Feminism, Foucault and the Politics of the Body," in Price and Shildrick, *Feminist Theory and the Body*, 246–57.

41 My colleague David Pooler, a social work professor, studies the difficult subject of clergy sex abuse. He shares a treatment strategy for survivors in this coauthored paper: David K. Pooler and Amanda Frey, "Responding to Survivors of Clergy Sexual Abuse," in *Treating Trauma in Christian Counseling*, ed. Heather Davediuk Gingrich and Fred C. Gingrich (Downers Grove, IL: InterVarsity, 2017), 188–210.

42 Mary's pregnancy suffered, in Gaventa's words, its own "taint of scandal" (*Mary: Glimpses*, 38).

43 See Llywelyn, "Mirror of Justice," 286.

44 Paul VI, *Marialis Cultus: For the Right Ordering and Development of Devotion to the Blessed Virgin Mary*, Holy See, February 2, 1974, https://tinyurl.com/nkahwdua, 18.

45 Llywelyn, "Mirror of Justice," 287.

46 Llywelyn, 287–88.

47 Murphy, "Omnipotent by Grace," 192.

48 Llywelyn, "Mirror of Justice," 288.

49 Murphy, "Omnipotent by Grace," 195. Francisco Suarez embeds or, to be precise, embodies her goodness in her womb.

50 I am sympathetic to this view. Feminist phenomenologists demonstrate the significant role of the body in both having and understanding phenomenal experiences. The recent groundswell of theories about the body have generated robust analyses of embodiment that aid feminist work. I draw on theories of the body in my article "Relationality and Life: Phenomenological Reflections on Miscarriage" to explain and elevate women's material phenomenology, citing the work of Rosalyn Diprose, *The Bodies of Women: Ethics, Embodiment and Sexual Difference* (London: Routledge, 1994); Moira Gatens, *Imaginary Bodies: Ethics, Power and Corporeality* (London: Routledge, 1996); Moira Gatens, "Beauvoir and Biology: A Second Look," in *The Cambridge Companion to Simone de Beauvoir*, ed. Claudia Card (Cambridge: Cambridge University Press, 2006), 266–85; Elizabeth Grosz, *Volatile Bodies: Toward a Corporeal Feminism* (Bloomington: Indiana University Press, 1994); Elizabeth A. Grosz, *Space, Time, and Perversion: Essays on the Politics of Bodies* (London: Routledge, 1995); and Lisa Guenther, *The Gift of the Other: Levinas and the Politics of Reproduction* (Albany: State University of New York Press, 2006), among others.

51 I regularly read and teach Andrea Dworkin's radical feminist text *Intercourse*. I admire the ferocity of her language, the sheer force of her diction, the incisiveness of her words to name and illustrate the visceral qualities of sexual intercourse (penetrating, invading, thrusting), and the way she exposes the insidious side of intercourse for women: male domination. I find myself compelled by her insight that intercourse has a political meaning (intercourse denotes women's fundamental lack of privacy) and signifies women's lower human status (women lack metaphysical integrity and, therefore, self-respect): "Can an occupied people—physically occupied inside, internally invaded—be free; can those with a metaphysically compromised privacy have self-determination; can those without a biologically based physical integrity have self-respect?" (124). I am drawn, haltingly and hauntingly, to her arguments that the status of women is inextricably bound up with the use of their bodies (for sexual gratification—or, as she puts it, for invasion, for occupation—and, either intentionally

or accidentally, reproduction). As she sees it—and as I think I, too, see it—the insidious process of female objectification results in self-negation: "There is the initial complicity, the acts of self-mutilation, self-diminishing, self-reconstruction, until there is no self, only the diminished, mutilated reconstruction. It is all superficial and unimportant, except what it costs the human in her to do it: except for the fact that it is submissive, conforming, giving up an individuality that would withstand object status or defy it" (141). It is difficult to resist Dworkin's claim that female objectification leads to self-negation and alienation when analyzing feminine archetypes like Mary in the blinding light of patriarchal power. Objectification is "the best system of colonization on earth: she takes on the burden, the responsibility, of her own submission, her own objectification" (142).

52 Murphy, "Omnipotent by Grace," 201. The Augustinian tradition, stressing the choice of maternity, is preferable to the Suarezian view, which accentuates biological motherhood, because her assent is personal, and it is by virtue of this personal act that she is the mother of unique persons. So this is where her personality, the locus of her omnipotence, resides in her unbounded assent to mothering the church.

53 Figurative pregnancies—women's birthing of ideas, systems, and institutions— can ameliorate the masculine marking of intellectual and spiritual activities that enforce female subordination.

54 David Gibson, "Christmas' Missing Icon: Mary Breastfeeding Jesus," *Washington Post*, December 10, 2012, https://tinyurl.com/ah7zmfm.

55 Julie Fiore's pithy explanation of color-coded attire in Christian art (Mary in blue and Jesus in red) contains an important gender element: "Still, today, the balance of red and blue, male and female, remains key to upholding Christian-defined gender norms—traditions we don't seem fully yet able to let go of. Whereas in an earlier age, the color-coding of Jesus and Mary linked red to masculinity and blue to femininity, values that eventually flipped. But who knows where the symbolic meanings of these colors will take us in the future as we continue to evolve our ideas about gender roles, religion, and art." Julia Fiore, "Why Jesus and Mary Always Wear Red and Blue in Art History," Artsy, December 19, 2018, https://tinyurl.com/dm8t4ajr.

56 Margaret Rose Realy, "Walnuts, Thanksgiving, and a Garden Catechism," Patheos, November 14, 2014, https://tinyurl.com/2yvmxjkh. Christ's association with walnuts symbolizes his divine nature and fruitfulness in ministry. Incidentally, Mary's association with milk has lost its positive signification and now connotes her immanent (and sexual) bodily nature and a subversion of the pure, spiritual nourishment she once symbolized.

57 Realy.

58 Miri Rubin, *Mother of God: A History of the Virgin Mary* (New Haven, CT: Yale University Press, 2009), 207–12. Rubin maintains that artistic representations of Mary and the Christ child aim to communicate the Christian story to diverse lay audiences through elements of their family life. Thus the scenes and mode of attachment between Mary and Jesus change over time. In the thirteenth century, static representations gave way to gestures that communicated emotion, a "new style of representation engaged with movement and hinted at a narrative" (205). Regional styles shaped mother-son representation. *Maria lactans* representations decline near the end of the thirteenth century as the breast (and nudity) becomes abject. Reflective of this shift, representations of Mary as a "beautiful, feminine figure, with long locks of hair and a graceful body portrayed in movement and gesture" and a flawless face with smooth skin include "attention to her breasts" (211), especially in poetry. "Source of food and nurture, the breast was a sign of Mary's love. Since Mary cared for all Christians she was imagined as baring her breast when she pleaded for sinners" (211). The logical move from physical to emotional (and perhaps libidinous) sustenance emerges strongly in thirteenth-century art: "Mary's material motherhood, as taught and shown in images and words, led poets to explore desire at its utmost: they created poetry which saw love, food, and nurture combined at Mary's breast" (211). For example, Werner the Swiss's poem "Marienleben" depicts Jesus as longing to return to Mary's womb: "Here [in the poem] is the astonishing suggestion that God so loved being a baby at the breast, even a foetus in the womb, that he sought to re-enter Mary's body and unmake the Incarnation! The poet imagines the fulfillment of the desire for Mary's breast in Jesus' return to it and into Mary's body. Others imagined that return in fantasies of oneness with Mary" (212). By the fourteenth century, artists transform Mary

from a bodily mother concerned for her child's (and audiences')
spiritual nourishment to a docile mother concerned for her child's
(and audiences') moral education: "Chaste and docile, reading her
book, Mary of the thirteenth and fourteenth centuries is an ideal
type for young womanhood: accepting, obedient, beautiful and full
of grace" (214). Sermons of the late fourteenth century emphasized
Mary's purity and reinforced her image as a "settled" (215) mother.

59   Realy, "Walnuts."

60   Gibson, "Christmas' Missing Icon."

61   Gibson.

62   Gibson.

63   Gibson.

64   Gibson. The sacrifice of the cross—the suffering Jesus—became the
dominant motif of Christianity while the Nativity "was sanitized
into a Hallmark card" for the Christmas season. Gibson appeals to
the work of Margaret Miles, *A Complex Delight: The Secularization
of the Breast, 1350–1750* (Berkeley: University of California Press,
2008), to argue that, during the Renaissance, the crucifixion displaced Mary's breast as the major symbol of God's love for humanity
(Gibson, "Christmas' Missing Icon").

65   Gibson, "Christmas' Missing Icon."

66   Llywelyn, "Mirror of Justice," 288.

67   Bartky, "Foucault," 476. It is important to recall the powerful in-
ternalization of the feminine performance of subjectivity and, thus,
women's resistance to dismantling, as Bartky describes: "Any political project that aims to dismantle the machinery that turns a female
body into a feminine one may well be apprehended by a woman as
something that threatens her with desexualization, if not outright
annihilation" (476).

68   Elizabeth Fletcher, "Mary in Nazareth—the Real Woman," Women
in the Bible, 2006, https://tinyurl.com/bhw9u82s.

69   Gaventa in *Mary: Glimpses of the Mother of Jesus* mentions Mary's
other children. I suspect the christotypical reading of Mary and
singular focus on Jesus explain the children's invisibility, but I am
intrigued by their absence nonetheless. Parents of children with
different degrees of ableness can appreciate the subtle social erasure
of their less abled children. Jesus's specialness, a positive signification, operates in a similar way. Also, this image raises questions
about the status and treatment of stepparents, transgender parents,

and same-sex parents: parents who do not necessarily birth but nonetheless parent children. Nurturing, disciplining, teaching, and protecting children—are these inherently gendered activities?

70 Gaventa, *Mary: Glimpses*, 8.

71 Mary's status as a subject is of critical feminist concern. I urge you to read Jane Schaberg's analysis of Mariology in the epilogue to *The Illegitimacy of Jesus* as well as Beverly Gaventa's engagement with Schaberg and others as she, too, negotiates Mary's status as a subject in *Mary: Glimpses of the Mother of Jesus*. In brief, Schaberg rejects Rosemary Radford Ruether's attempt to save Mary from "carnal sexuality and reproduction" (Schaberg, *Illegitimacy*, 198; through a unification with the Holy Spirit and flight from the mortal body) because of the persistent sexism surrounding Mariology. Schaberg's alternative is to embrace and integrate Jesus's illegitimacy (and Mary's deviance) to produce a Mary that is liberated from oppression: "a woman who has access to the sacred outside the patriarchal family and its control" (Schaberg, 199). Gaventa observes the similarities and differences among feminist scholars on the point of Mary and concludes that, at least for the Roman Catholic tradition, Mary's place and status in the church are undergoing a reexamination (Gaventa, *Mary: Glimpses*, 14). Gaventa expresses skepticism about Schaberg's argument from silence (Gaventa, 14; Schaberg, 199) and concludes from her literary analysis (Gaventa, 11) that Mary exhibits signs of agency as a vulnerable, faithful, and *reflecting* subject who initiates Christian reflection (Gaventa, 130).

72 Our Lady of Guadalupe, also known as the Virgin of Guadalupe, is a Catholic title of the Blessed Virgin Mary associated with a series of five Marian apparitions in December 1531. She is a venerated image on a cloak enshrined within the Basilica of Our Lady of Guadalupe in Mexico City. *Encyclopaedia Britannica Online*, s.v. "Our Lady of Guadalupe," last modified May 15, 2020, https://tinyurl.com/9sfu9yvs.

73 Reimagining Mary in this aesthetic vein challenges misogynistic and racist readings of the womb as a white, sacred, public, politically charged space. Beyoncé's appropriation of Mary's power subverts the church's complicity in racial oppression.

74 I am grateful to Craig Clarkson, Christopher Richmann, Andrew Arterbury, and Douglas Weaver for providing helpful insights into the concept of womb as divine, immaterial space. Christians,

especially evangelical Protestants, believe Scripture also provides support for seeing the womb as divine space and legitimating opposition to abortion.

75 For a Christian analysis of the trending *#blessed*, see Jason Tucker, "#Blessed: What Jesus Really Says about It," *Jason Tucker* (blog), February 18, 2019, https://www.jasontucker.faith/blessed/.

76 I appreciate my many conversations with Christopher Richmann about the Marian archetype and his generous insights about the cultural manifestations of womb as sacred space. I find the Marian signification of contemporary pregnancy fascinating.

77 Amy Mullin, *Reconceiving Pregnancy and Childcare: Ethics, Experience, and Reproductive Labor* (Cambridge: Cambridge University Press, 2005), 63.

78 Llywelyn, "Mirror of Justice," 290.

Chapter 2

1 Thomas Laqueur, *Making Sex: Body and Gender from the Greeks to Freud* (Cambridge, MA: Harvard University Press, 1994); and Nicole Loraux, *The Children of Athena: Athenian Ideas about Citizenship and the Division between the Sexes*, trans. Caroline Levine (Princeton, NJ: Princeton University Press, 1993) offer insightful analyses of femininity over and against concepts like "woman" and "female." Loraux points out that the mythology surrounding the birth of Athens affirms both "the defeat of women and the victory of the feminine" (*Children of Athena*, 11). She argues that Athens adopts the misogyny of Hesiod but also embraces the myth of Pandora. Athens thus makes room for a race of females while excluding real women from citizenship and political practice. Because Athena oversees the birth (and rearing) of Pandora, she watches over the fertility of Athens by providing divine security for the male, the hero, and the citizen. Although she is "a figure impossible in the human world," her mythic association with Pandora allows the feminine to haunt "the Athenian civic imagination, which never succeeds in separating the goddess from the women of Athens" (11).

2 Apollodorus (Pseudo-Apollodorus) recounts the story of Athena's birth in *The Library*, or *Bibliotheca*, a second-century BCE text. Zeus swallows Metis, his first wife and the Titan goddess of

wisdom, having been warned she will threaten his power. Metis is pregnant with their daughter Athena. Metis sets to work inside Zeus's head and crafts Athena a set of protective armor. The clamor of her work causes Zeus a debilitating headache. His pain becomes so unbearable that Prometheus (or Hephaestus) strikes Zeus's head with an ax, a welcoming rupturing that births Athena. Athena is neither born from a woman nor gives birth herself. Apollodorus, *Apollodorus' Library and Hyginus' Fabulae: Two Handbooks of Greek Mythology*, trans. R. Scott Smith and Stephen M. Trzaskoma (Indianapolis, IN: Hackett, 2007).

3 Philip Mayerson, *Classical Mythology in Literature, Art, and Music* (Newburyport, MA: Focus, 2001), 171.

4 Joan Breton Connelly, *Portrait of a Priestess: Women and Ritual in Ancient Greece* (Princeton, NJ: Princeton University Press, 2007), 63. Connelly maintains that the role of Greek priestesses to various cult statues, including *Athena Polias* at Athens, gave women a valuable public role in Athenian communities that yielded more agency than previously believed (5).

5 Connelly, 4–5.

6 Connelly, 2–4.

7 Loraux, *Children of Athena*, xiv.

8 Loraux, 11.

9 Connelly, *Portrait*, 41, 59. Simone de Beauvoir strikes an Athenian note in the 1950s by rejecting marriage and motherhood for the sake of philosophical and political work. Women cannot, in her view, take care of men and children and pursue independent goals and interests.

10 Athena materializes the threat of the masculine woman that still lingers today. Mary Wollstonecraft makes explicit the (male) fear of a manly woman in *A Vindication of the Rights of Woman: With Strictures on Political and Moral Subjects*, ed. D. L. Macdonald and Kathleen Scherf (Peterborough, ON: Broadview, 1997). Thomas Laqueur acknowledges the historic binary that divides male and female behavior and makes impossible the reality of a feminine man or masculine woman (*Making Sex*, 8).

11 My colleague Anne-Marie Schultz, an esteemed Plato scholar and author of *Plato's Socrates as Narrator: A Philosophical Muse* (Lanham, MD: Lexington Books, 2013) and *Plato's Socrates on Socrates: Socratic Self-Disclosure and the Public Practice of Philosophy* (Lanham, MD: Lexington Books, 2020), points out that Plato's *Republic* shows an awareness of women "functioning" as men. Also, the

wonderful female figure Diotima in Plato's *Symposium* gives birth to ideas of beauty. Although I offer a modern appropriation of Athena in this chapter and argue throughout the book that archetypal figures have purchase because they mirror the realities of real women, Anne has nicely reminded me how much Greek scholars enjoy exploring Athena's function as a model of womanhood in ancient contexts. I have folded in some references to Joan Breton Connelly's work on priestesses and Athena's role therein. I would also recommend Page duBois's work, which is filled with fascinating links between ancient culture and the modern psyche.

12　Conformity comes in different packages. Submission, assimilation, sublimation, and subversion are among them, as the archetypes featured here, respectively, illustrate.

13　Becoming a wife and mother entails an embodiment of roles and functions that bear low social and economic value—for example, rearing children, cleaning domestic spaces, and preparing meals—and, for some, less fulfillment than professional activities. The reality of female subjugation drives Woolf's *A Room of One's Own*. I deploy Virginia Woolf's metaphor of a "room" to represent female freedom from male constraint and social oppression throughout my analysis of archetypal forms of female agency and identity. Whereas Woolf conceives of woman's freedom as an external, social exercise of freedom, I argue that a woman's body is the "room" or situation in which her freedom is realized. Freedom is thus an internal, material expression of identity as well as a sociotemporal experience of unrestraint. Woman's embodied womb compromises her efforts to achieve equality. Virginia Woolf, *A Room of One's Own* (New York: Harcourt, Brace, 1929).

14　Woolf, 199.

15　Apollodorus, *Library*.

16　Chris Moffett, "About," *Splitting Skulls* (blog), Columbia University, March 26, 2010, https://blogs.cuit.columbia.edu/cm2189/tag/zeus/.

17　Loraux, *Children of Athena*, 9.

18　Mary Wollstonecraft aptly notes the gendered dimension of man's fear of empowered women, *the masculine woman*, in her eighteenth-century feminist text, *A Vindication of the Rights of Woman*. Man's fear of impotence—loss of power, loss of control, and fear of erasure—hovers over, and shapes the resistance to, female equality then and now.

19 Londa Schiebinger traces the history of woman's presumed nature and status in *Nature's Body: Gender in the Making of Modern Science*. Schiebinger maintains that woman's assumed lack of male rationality and bodily strength is an ancient one: "Among all the organs of a woman's body, her reproductive organs were considered most animal-like." Londa Schiebinger, *Nature's Body: Gender in the Making of Modern Science* (New Brunswick, NJ: Rutgers University Press, 2010), 55.

20 Prehistoric fertility cults, on one end, and contemporary Facebook baby bump photos, on the other, bookend the degree to which woman's identity is tied to her reproductive success.

21 The Venus of Willendorf exemplifies the cultic commitment to woman's reproductivity.

22 Audre Lorde proves the weakness of the view that woman's equality depends on a recognition of her rationality in "The Master's Tools Will Never Dismantle the Master's House," in *Sister Outsider* (Trumansburg, NY: Crossing, 1984). The (male) mind does nothing to dismantle the masculine construction of femininity because the disciplining of the body resists mind's messages that the body is insignificant.

23 Joan Breton Connelly argues that while ancient Greek female priestesses may represent submissive, disempowered women who are subjugated by the male gaze, there is evidence to suggest that women priestesses were not powerless. Indeed, they realized "genuine accomplishment through their agency within the system," a system in which women were indispensable (*Portrait*, 20).

24 Connelly, 2.

25 Aristophanes, *Lysistrata*, trans. Dudley Fitts (New York: Harcourt, Brace, 1954). Lysistrata initiates an oath among women around the wine cup that they shall have nothing to do with their husbands and lovers in protest of war (16–19).

26 Loraux, *Children of Athena*, 10–11. Loraux observes that "the political process does not recognize a 'citizeness,' the language has no word for a woman from Athens" (10).

27 Connelly, *Portrait*, 3.

28 Loraux, *Children of Athena*, 247–48.

29 Woolf, *Room of One's Own*, 188. Woolf argues that "intellectual freedom depends upon material things." Women have enjoyed less freedom "than the sons of Athenians slaves" (188) because of their lack of economic and physical freedom. Woolf materializes the reality of women through the figure of Judith, the gifted, imaginary

sister of Shakespeare. When Judith, who is a "genius . . . for fiction," realizes she is with child, she takes her own life (83–84). Woolf concludes that a woman born with intellectual gifts in the sixteenth century "would certainly have gone crazed, shot herself, or ended her days in some lonely cottage" (85).

30 An external reader asked the excellent question of whether it is true that there is no Athena archetype in the Euro-American cultural and civic imagination or whether, instead, the respectability of women like Hillary Clinton, Margaret Thatcher, Elizabeth Warren, Golda Meir, and Indira Gandhi is challenged because of the way that they subvert seemingly essential parts of womanhood (sexuality, motherhood) in favor of their identity as rational, asexual, male-like professionals. I appreciate this call for clarification. The difficulty with these examples is that all five women are married with children. So even when their femininity is questioned by opponents to gain political advantage—or even when they themselves bracket the feminine elements of their lives for the sake of professional duties—they nonetheless embody womanhood in normative ways, ways that enable them and their supporters to push back on opponents, challenge male leaders, and maintain authority among women. Kamala Harris, who is married with stepchildren but no biological children, may provide an alternative case for consideration. My larger claim, however, is that Euro-Americans are not culturally able to affirm "as a woman" a female who chooses celibacy for the sake of career because our shared understanding of woman is bound up with wombed, domestic activities and meanings. I hope I am wrong.

31 Schiebinger explains how eighteenth-century women are defined by reproduction while eighteenth-century men are defined by "physical strength, skin color, or intelligence" (*Nature's Body*, 6–7).

32 Judith G. Coffin, *Sex, Love, and Letters: Writing Simone de Beauvoir* (Ithaca, NY: Cornell University Press, 2020), 54.

33 Hannah Arendt, *The Human Condition*, 2nd ed. (Chicago: University of Chicago Press, 1998), 12.

34 Arendt, 7.

35 Arendt, 58.

36 Connelly acknowledges the ambiguity and complexity of male and female identity. To be female in antiquity incorporates the wisdom of the "masculine" warrior and craftsman Athena (Connelly, *Portrait*, 30).

37 The Panathenia was an annual celebration in honor of Athena on the occasion of her birthday. It included religious activities, such as clothing Athena statues in new garbs, and athletic competitions. Amphoras were given as prizes; the Burgon vase was a prize for a chariot race. This representation of Athena in combat pose is typical of these Panatheniac prize amphoras.

38 I am grateful to Heidi Bostic for mentioning Luce Irigaray's work on the genealogy of Jesus where she focuses on Mary's mother, Anne, and her human qualities.

39 Informal workplace language often responds to the threat of the masculine woman with humor. A woman academic at another institution gave me a name plate for my desk that reads "Boss Lady."

40 Susan Bordo describes the process of disciplinary feminization in her 2003 essay, "The Empire of Images in Our World of Bodies," *The Chronicle of Higher Education*, December 19, 2003, https:// tinyurl.com/3jvwkx8h.

41 I am grateful to my former colleague and historian Jacqueline-Bethel Mougoué for pointing out that in the Global South, motherhood and politics of the womb "give" you power and the right to engage in politics and to "mother" and condemn male political elites who commit wrongdoing.

42 I thank Danielle Hansen for making this excellent point and supplying these apt examples.

43 Many feminine activities revolve around children. And feminine activities, such as cooking and laundry, are much more valued and central to daily life when one has growing children to nourish and clothe.

44 Anne Fausto-Sterling, "Menopause: The Storm before the Calm," in *Feminist Theory and the Body: A Reader*, ed. Janet Price and Margrit Shildrick (New York: Routledge, 2010), 169.

45 In an August 10, 2009, blog article titled "Unbelievable Feminista Hogwash about Quality Husbands," Dr. Laura writes, "There are biological and psychological imperatives in females for nesting/childcare, and in males for conquering/protecting. When these are turned inside out, there is usually (but not always) a reaction in the female to feel less respectful and sexual toward her mate. . . . Women who want emasculated men generally have huge hostility issues with masculinity (which they got from their mothers or the feminist teachers of their women's studies courses) and want to be able to control the man (never as much as their mother could)

or are just too scared of their normal natural dependency on a real man." Laura Schlessinger, "Unbelievable Feminista Hogwash about Quality Husbands," *Dr. Laura* (blog), August 10, 2009, quoted and referenced in Byard Duncan, "Dr. Laura Schlessinger," Generation Progress, Center for American Progress, September 9, 2010, https://genprogress.org/dr-laura-schlessinger/.

46 Implicit and explicit critiques of working women have dominated media news since the end of World War II.

47 Wollstonecraft raises the specter and fear of the masculine woman in the introduction to *A Vindication of the Rights of Woman* (74–78).

48 Loraux, *Children of Athena*, 75.

49 Loraux, 75.

50 Loraux, 75.

51 Loraux, 73.

52 Euripides refers to Athena as a "goddess without a mother" (Loraux, 128).

53 Schiebinger observes that "the male body remained the touchstone of human anatomy" in eighteenth-century Europe (*Nature's Body*, 160). Men were also differentiated from women by their ability to reason, speak, and create culture (94).

54 I again thank Jacque Mougoué for emphasizing the exclusionary nature of Euro-American culture.

55 The premise of both *The Feminine Mystique* and *The Second Sex* is that women, particularly college-educated women, seek to be more than wives and mothers. See Betty Friedan, *The Feminine Mystique* (New York: W. W. Norton, 1963); and Simone de Beauvoir, *The Second Sex*, trans. Constance Borde and Shiela Malovany-Chevallier (London: Jonathan Cape, 2009).

56 Laqueur, *Making Sex*, 22.

57 Laqueur, 11.

58 Laqueur, 8.

59 Laqueur, 8, 10–11.

60 Laqueur, 20.

61 Connelly, *Portrait*, 5.

62 Connelly, 5.

63 Connelly, 5–6.

64 Connelly, 41.

65 Loraux, *Children of Athena*, 11.

66 Loraux, 11.

67 Laqueur, *Making Sex*, 15–16.

68 Laqueur, 8.

69 Laqueur, 8.

70 Laqueur, 12.

71 Miri Rubin reflects on the material work of Mary in *Mother of God: A History of the Virgin Mary* (New Haven, CT: Yale University Press, 2009). The Italian monk Anselm of Lucca (1036–86 CE), for example, emphasizes Mary's unmediated, unparalleled access to and experience of Christ's body (134–35).

72 Gibson, "Christmas' Missing Icon."

73 Schiebinger, *Nature's Body*, 69.

74 Schiebinger notes that "eighteenth-century politics became body politics *par excellence*" insofar as the laws of nature shaped the laws of the state (9).

75 The first wave of colonization beginning in the fifteenth century generated new interest in science as objects from Eastern lands made their ways back to European ports.

76 Deanna Petherbridge and Ludmilla Jordanova rightly maintain that anatomical drawings are concerned with "the 'mapping' of the body, which is perhaps why, since the 16th century, they have been called atlases." *The Quick and the Dead: Artists and Anatomy* (Berkeley: University of California Press, 1997), 63.

77 Susan Wendell's argument for transcendence with body applies well to differently abled bodies and women's bodies insofar as neither community can escape the embodied situation that defines their lived experiences. "Feminism, Disability, and the Transcendence of the Body," in Price and Shildrick, *Feminist Theory and the Body*, 332.

78 Hannah Arendt invokes the stereotypical western understanding of gender and the public/private distinction in *The Human Condition*, where she aligns women with the labor of the home and men with the action of the polis. In reality, Arendt's true "action" isn't really even possible at all anymore, as we now lack a true "public sphere"—all we have is the confusing mush of "society."

Chapter 3

1 Oskar Seyffert, *A Dictionary of Classical Antiquities,* ed. Henry Nettleship and J. E. Sandys (New York: Meridian, 1956), 681.

2 Seyffert, 681. Ginette Paris rightly asserts that "the numerous myths concerning the birth of Aphrodite vary according to epoch,

ideology, and place of origin." *Pagan Meditations: The Worlds of Aphrodite, Artemis, and Hestia,* trans. Gwendolyn Moore (Dallas: Spring, 1987), 12. Yet the use and mix of many variants is appropriate for nonhistorians and non-Hellenists who seek not to re-create a historical lineage but rather to problematize different aspects of our consciousness related to Aphrodite myths.

3 *The Birth of Venus (Nascita di Venere)* is a late fifteenth-century painting by the Italian artist Sandro Botticelli. Botticelli's enormously sensual presentation of the goddess Venus arriving at shore after her birth from the sea is highly accessible and popular. See Sandro Botticelli, *Birth of Venus,* ca. 1485, tempera on canvas, Le Gallerie Degli Uffizi, Florence, Italy, https://www.uffizi.it/en/artworks/birth-of-venus.

4 Michael Macrone, *Brush Up Your Mythology!* (New York: Gramercy, 1999), 25, 27. Ginette Paris points out the aptness of Athena's and Aphrodite's functions given their origins. The strong and intellectual Athena is born from the head of Zeus, whereas the sexy Aphrodite is born from her father's genitals (*Pagan Meditations,* 15). Caelus's loss of power is a symbol of death.

5 Macrone, *Brush Up,* 27. Also, like the foam that forms her, Venus stirs up lust or "venery," a derivative of her name (27).

6 Venus embodies the absurdity of female subjectivity, the illogical construct of femininity.

7 Seyffert, *Classical Antiquities,* 681. Seyffert reports that Venus's earliest Roman name was *Murcĭa,* later interpreted as *Myrtĕa,* goddess of myrtles, which ties her to the Greek goddess Aphrodite. The first historical mention of her worship appears in this form in 217 BCE (681).

8 Paris, *Pagan Meditations,* 13. Paris is quoting Charlene Spretnak here.

9 Civil and political stability requires a suspension of sexual woman because sex is destabilizing (recall *Lysistrata*). Yet psychic stability and interior self-order—a management of self—require sexual woman, which is also apparent in *Lysistrata.* The paradox of sex problematizes female subjectivity.

10 Venus, like Athena and Barbie, stands apart from Mary for another reason. She (they) lack Mary's ontological status—that is, Athena, Venus, and Barbie are archetypal representations of (different) women rather than real women. Because they did not exist in real

life, their stories are produced purely out of a collective cultural imagination, whereas Mary's story—the dominant voices that constructed and codified Mary's story over time—grew out of a historical event in Mary's life that she herself did not write down or interpret. Certainly, the ontological difference between Mary and the other female icons explored here matters; Mary's lived experience matters for theological and historical reasons among others. But in an important (dare one say essential) sense—a sense isolated in this book—female archetypes have purchase because they mirror real women. Their iconographic force, the nearly totalizing power they exert in women's lives and identities, transcends their ontological difference. Female archetypes personify performances of woman by real women; each icon points to a negative valence (patriarchy trying to dictate women's identities) and a positive valence (each archetype subverting patriarchy), an opposition that invites women to resist patriarchal imaginings of womanhood, expand the idea and experience of wombed persons, and reclaim the subject status and authority to perform woman in new ways. I am grateful to Danielle Hansen for prompting me to address whether archetypal performances of woman have power because they arise from the lives of real women or because they mirror real women. I maintain the latter view without, I hope, diminishing the examples of real women.

11 A contemporary appropriation of Venus's spiritual elevation of sex might benefit women because women are typically viewed as the source of male moral failure—that is, women's erotic power over men corrupts women.

12 Humans approximate immortality through the reproduction of children or through the creation of a life that leaves a lingering impression or lasting difference for future generations. Sex recalls the experience of something beyond the self, beyond the banality of life, and beyond the present moment.

13 I acknowledge the heteronormative presentation of sex within the Venus story's focus of reproduction as a sublimating tool for male aggression. Venus's interest in emotional connection and physical pleasure, however, opens up space for nonnormative sexualities. Her layered emphases mark her paradoxically as a figure who both affirms and subverts sexual norms.

14 Venus's creation account contributes to the marking of women as corrupting, sexual creatures.

15 See Paris, *Pagan Meditations*, 15, for a deeper analysis of the contrast between Athena and Aphrodite.

16 Paris deploys the phrase "fertilizing unions" (15).

17 The disappearance of Mary's breasts in Christian iconography occurs in the sixteenth century following the Council of Trent's concern about the nude body and the mass production of printed, pornographic materials. Margaret R. Miles offers a rich analysis of the breast in modern art and culture in *A Complex Delight: The Secularization of the Breast, 1350–1750*. For a fun, fact-filled examination of the "natural and unnatural" history of the breast, check out Florence Williams, *Breasts: A Natural and Unnatural History* (New York: W. W. Norton, 2012).

18 Paris, *Pagan Meditations*, 14–15. Caelus's claiming of the birthing process for himself parallels Zeus's birthing of Athena. Similarly, his assignation of Venus's sexualized signification and function arises from her creation from his genitals. Athena is born from Zeus's head. Hence their respective sexual and intellectual prowess.

19 Paris, 18.

20 Andrea Dworkin, *Intercourse*, 20th anniversary ed. (New York: Basic Books, 2007) is a text that offers honest, irreducible insight into the female condition despite its fatalistic feel. Whereas Dworkin regards intercourse as immune to reform in a male-dominant world, Venus presents sexuality as a path to female liberation through a reserve power move that subdues man and empowers woman. I will confess that I am sympathetic to Dworkin's view, but I recognize the potential of Venus to reform sexual practices, a potential that contemporary feminists find attractive.

21 Venus's motivation for uniting woman and man parallels Athena's aim in creating the polis. Venus propagates life amid the perpetual threat of death and destruction as Athena protects law and order against forces that threaten to undermine the peace and prosperity her safeguards ensure. Psychically, the child sublimates the father's desire to dominate and subordinate the mother (as symbolized by Caelus's and Saturn's actions) and transforms the father's self-love and self-interest into paternalism—the love, support, and protection of the child's nurturing mother and the child herself. The mother regains power through the production of a child.

22 Venus represents an advancement of the pregnant female subject, a progressive counterpoint to both Mary and Athena.

23 Straight, cisgender dads can perform "motherly" childcare duties without fearing a loss of male authority if these duties no longer hold a female signification—that is, if soothing, feeding, and nurturing children is not a female-exclusive or feminine-coded activity. Similarly, transgender parents can care for their children without compromising their gender identities if childcare duties lose their gendered (male and female) significations. In this way, heterosexual, cisgender men can come to appreciate the plight of transgender parents.

24 Joanna Ebenstein, *The Anatomical Venus* (London: Thames & Hudson, 2016), 28–29.

25 Virginia L. Campbell, "Something Old, Something New," *Pompeian Connections: Networks in Pompeii and the Roman World* (blog), September 6, 2016, https://pompeiinetworks.wordpress .com/page/4/. A pearl's formation is not unlike human development with its slow, painstaking maturation of an embryo within the soft tissue of a mother's womb. Nor is pearl formation unlike Venus's personal, painful origin and erotic performance of pregnancy: she emerges from a castrated phallus and in turn symbolically castrates men.

26 Venus sublimates male aggression, subdues psychic angst, and unites men and women through sexual intimacy and reproduction.

27 Wollstonecraft seeks to distance woman from her sexual identity in *A Vindication of the Rights of Woman* by strengthening her identity as mother, an identification with virtue. While Wollstonecraft's efforts enhance woman's intellectual and moral coding, they also increase the stigma of the sexual woman by placing sexuality and motherhood in distinct spheres of feminine activity with sexuality in a subordinate, degraded position.

28 The Venus representation of sexuality (re)casts female desire in a positive, productive light, a light subsequently distinguished by repressive constructs of female sexuality. We need to reconsider sex's constructive ends, including its psychic dimensions, but our reconsideration must take place in the context of our culture's objectification of women. Simone de Beauvoir's structuralist account of man as the ideal human and woman as the Other, a cultural alien subjugated by her inert womb, in *The Second Sex*, expresses an important but incomplete picture of woman. See Beauvoir, *Second Sex*.

29 Dworkin, *Intercourse*. Dworkin describes the use and abuse of women's bodies in intercourse in chapter 7, "Occupation/Collaboration." A woman's bodily "hole" or "slit" between her legs is synonymous with entry, Dworkin argues, an opening that compromises her privacy, her dignity, and her significance for material rather than social reasons (155).

30 Judith G. Coffin expands on the work of Michel Bozon by describing a "variable geometry" of sexuality with its "crisscrossing lines and circles that connect the overlapping domains of body, psyche, emotions, identity, motives, desires, social relations, and culture" under the "nearly incoherent subject" of sex. The term *sex* has been supplanted by a plurality of terms—gender, gender roles, sex, and sexuality—that theorize sex in a multiplicity of ways and produce "little chance of stabilizing the volatility of 'sex' and its implications" to this day. Judith G. Coffin, *Sex, Love, and Letters: Writing Simone de Beauvoir* (Ithaca, NY: Cornell University Press, 2020), 54, 60, respectively.

31 Coffin, 62.

32 Coffin, 62.

33 Laura Mulvey's still formidable, Freudian analysis of the male gaze in "Visual Pleasure and Narrative Cinema" aptly captures woman's erotic coding in the matrix of male power. She writes, "In a world ordered by sexual imbalance, pleasure in looking has been split between active/male and passive/female. The determining male gaze projects its fantasy onto the female figure, which is styled accordingly. In their traditional exhibitionist role women are simultaneously looked at and displayed, with their appearance coded for strong visual and erotic impact so that they can be said to connote *to-be-looked-at-ness*. Woman displayed as sexual object is the *leitmotif* of erotic spectacle: from pin-ups to strip-tease, from Ziegfeld to Busby Berkeley, she holds the look, and plays to and signifies male desire." Laura Mulvey, "Visual Pleasure and Narrative Cinema," in *Visual and Other Pleasures* (Bloomington: Indiana University Press, 1989), 19.

34 I am recalling Sandra Lee Bartky's idea of a *produced* feminine body-subject, a production generated through normative, disciplinary practices that "produce a 'practiced and subjected' body, that is, a body on which an inferior status has been inscribed" ("Foucault," 472).

35 Recall that Mary's breasts are an important symbol of her nourishment of the church until they acquire an erotic signification. Also,

etymologically, "matrix" is linked to womb. In French, *la matrice* is the word for womb when used in anatomical (*anatomie*) contexts. Women's bodies, nude or clothed, are not responsible for women's sexual objectification. Sexual allure does not make a woman a sex object: beauty exists within a formal, higher order. Nor do historic, literary, and artistic representations of the female form objectify and sexualize body parts. Rather, the matrix of power in which women's and men's bodies operate, such as patriarchy and capitalism, determine the signification of sex and the assigned values of their respective labor.

36 This is especially true for pregnant women and mothers who are construed as nonsexual beings in the mold of the Marian archetype and thus experience themselves as undesirable, even unattractive. A desiring mother is a deviant mother.

37 Dworkin offers a Woolf echo in her analysis of women's poverty. She, however, extends women's poverty beyond economic, educational, and cultural poverty to psychic impoverishment: "We [women] are poorer than men in money and so we have to barter sex or sell it outright (which is why they keep us poorer in money). We are poorer than men in psychological well-being because for us self-esteem depends on the approval—frequently expressed through sexual desire—of those who have power over us" (Dworkin, *Intercourse*, 161). Dworkin goes on to argue that women have learned to "eroticize powerlessness" (174).

38 Like Kelly Oliver, I have a deep appreciation for Iris Marion Young's phenomenology of pregnant embodiment. Young reinstantiates the twin sides of Venus's legacy—female sexual desire and desexualized motherhood—in her articulation of pregnant subjectivity. But Oliver is right to worry that the dissolution of the border between sexuality and motherhood may not empower women to realize the self-love Young envisions. Indeed, Oliver declares that "Young's insistence that women's own experience of themselves as sexual subjects should be primary has not yet been realized within popular images of pregnancy." Kelly Oliver, *Knock Me Up, Knock Me Down: Images of Pregnancy in Hollywood Films* (New York: Columbia University Press, 2012), 37.

39 Emily Martin, "The Egg and the Sperm: How Science Has Constructed a Romance Based on Stereotypical Male-Female Roles," in Price and Shildrick, *Feminist Theory and the Body*, 179–89.

40 Dworkin, Ebenstein, and Oliver express this view in various ways. Oliver, for example, suggests that Hollywood represents pregnant bodies not as proud and liberated but rather as "sex objects for others" (*Knock Me Up*, 38).

41 Ebenstein traces the Anatomical Venus from a religious, instructional model to an erotic one, a "passive, life-sized doll created for men who prefer idealized surrogates to real women" (*Anatomical Venus*, 19).

42 In *Post-backlash Feminism*, Kellie Bean shows how the rise of regressive politics makes insidious claims on women's lives, undermines their social status, and limits their course of action. The effects of postfeminist feminism is power entwined with degradation: "This new feminism would organize itself around two goals: preserving patriarchy's access to the female body and 'saving the penis' from the castrating effects of old fashioned feminism." Kellie Bean, *Post-backlash Feminism: Women and the Media since Reagan-Bush* (Jefferson, NC: McFarland, 2007), 25.

43 Venus's sexual allure looks like desperate psychic coping when read through her family situation. Venus is an unwanted daughter born of an abused and alienated mother, dominant and explosive father, and protective but violent brother. Once sex loses its sacred signification, ecstasy is relegated to the physical realm.

44 For an examination of the ethical dimensions of reproductive labor, I encourage you to read Amy Mullin's *Reconceiving Pregnancy and Childcare*. Mullin's book served to encourage me to write this book.

45 Paris, *Pagan Meditations*, 73–77.

46 Paris, 28.

47 Ebenstein attributes the uncanniness of the Anatomical Venus to her realism. She challenges our basic understanding of reality and hurtles us "into a world of atavistic archetypes" (*Anatomical Venus*, 202).

48 Ebenstein, 18.

49 Ebenstein, 20–25.

50 Ebenstein, 28.

51 Ebenstein, 28.

52 Elizabeth Klaver, *Sites of Autopsy in Contemporary Culture* (Albany: State University of New York Press, 2005), 14.

53 Klaver, 26. When a female corpse is examined, the Y-incision is curved around the bottom of the breasts before meeting at the

breastbone. One might also draw a parallel between the image of Venus inside a shell, like a pearl once the shell is cracked open and the wax models (or other depictions) "cracked open" to view the organs inside.

54 Klaver, 14.

55 Many scholars note the prestige associated with the position of chief anatomist or "lecturer of anatomy" throughout Europe. Among them is T. V. N. Persaud, who notes in *The History of Anatomy* that the "lecturer of anatomy during the sixteenth and seventeenth centuries was a person of considerable importance and highly regarded." T. V. N. Persaud, Marios Loukas, and R. Shane Tubbs, *A History of Human Anatomy*, 2nd ed. (Springfield, IL: Charles C. Thomas, 2014), 54.

56 Persaud, 54.

57 Ebenstein mentions the Christian body and the role of wax in Christian rituals and traditions. Ebenstein, *Anatomical Venus*, 70–71.

58 Ebenstein, 18.

59 *Venerina* (Little Venus) is a 1782 life-size dissectible wax model created by the workshop of Clemente Susini at La Specola for Museo di Palazzo Poggi, Bologna, Italy. Ebenstein, *Anatomical Venus*, iii–iv.

60 Ebenstein, 28.

61 Ebenstein, 156–57. There were many intriguing automata in the early modern period; in the French context, one of the most famous is "Vaucanson's duck."

62 Deanna Petherbridge and Ludmilla Jordanova, *The Quick and the Dead: Artists and Anatomy* (Berkeley: University of California Press, 1997), 63.

63 Ebenstein, *Anatomical Venus*, 212–13.

64 Ebenstein, 202, 213.

65 Ebenstein, 150.

66 Ebenstein, 213.

67 Paris maintains that the loss of Venus's assurance of feminine beauty is an alienation of self in the performance of feminine activities: "As soon as feminine beauty loses its spiritual representation . . . women are enclosed within an infernal circle. . . . One cannot be against beauty, nor against virile strength. One would have to deny the beauty of flowers, of babies, and of children, birds and landscapes" (*Pagan Meditations*, 77). Although I am a monotheistic (Christian) feminist, I have tremendous regard for Paris's work and the invaluable dialogue about being a woman she initiates.

68 Venus's erotic performance of pregnant subjectivity raises additional, difficult questions about women's sexual habits and identity. How willing are women today to use their attractiveness and charm for personal advancement? How comfortable are women embodying Venus's practices of subversion and sublimation in light of the *#metoo* movement? Harvey Weinstein and Jeffrey Epstein? Sex trafficking? Title IX violations across college campuses? Female sexual harassment? Desacralization of sex? Impoverishment of intimacy? If Venus were situated in American culture today, would her sexual practices reinforce or resist female objectification? Oppress or liberate her? Empower or diminish her? Could her womb truly be hers—*could she enhance her desiring, agential, feminine performance of pregnant subjectivity as Young envisioned*—in the face of hedonistic, and often sadistic, carnal, sexual practices?

Chapter 4

1 J. Lenore Wright, "The Wonder of Barbie: Popular Culture and the Making of Female Identity," *Essays in Philosophy* 4, no. 1 (January 2003): 28–52. In this article, I analyze how female representation in popular culture shapes female identity. I begin by explicating the representational relationship among toys depicted as female, images of women in advertising, and televised representations of women. By adapting the analysis of games advanced by Kendall L. Walton in *Mimesis as Make-Believe: On the Foundations of the Representational Arts* (Cambridge, MA: Harvard University Press, 1990), I argue that Barbie qua representational female toy functions as a "prop" in the world of make-believe. As such, she allows children to explore identity without stipulating rules for identity formation, thereby encouraging them to play with their senses of self in an empowering way. Next, I examine the depiction and posturing of women in print advertising and compare female to male representation in the advertising world. I then discuss the challenges these images pose for self-identity, arguing that, unlike the games evoked by Barbie, advertising fosters a closed interpretative system, a system that promotes deterministic and negative views of women and female identity. Finally, I look briefly at key representations of women on television (dated and recent). I contend that, like

advertised representations of women, women of television are subject to a closed interpretative system that reads them against established female archetypes: nurturer, vixen, or victim. To combat the negative effects of these representations of women in advertising and on television, I argue that women must engage female representations in popular culture as children engage props in their imaginative games—as artifacts that coordinate but do not determine identity. By adopting an interpretative stance that invokes the sense of play and wonder present in games, we can create a space within the process of identity formation in which women can see (and read) themselves *not* as fixed objects within a closed system of commodification but instead as self-determining beings.

2 "Our History," About Barbie, Barbie.mattel.com, accessed November 26, 2020, https://tinyurl.com/4ejcjsju. Children can manipulate and move Barbie through space in ways that are impossible for two-dimensional dolls—Barbie can drive a car, for example. Barbie's realistic, representational form also expands children's vision of women's work and play. As they imagine and have Barbie perform activities like horseback riding, an absurdity for paper dolls, they envision new possibilities for real women.

3 "Our History."

4 Emma Bedford, "Gross Sales of Mattel's Barbie Brand Worldwide from 2012 to 2019 (in Millions of U.S. Dollars)," Statista, March 5, 2020, https://tinyurl.com/vwmfn9w7. All data about Barbie sales are located on this webpage. The following five data points come from this website.

5 Wright, "Wonder of Barbie," 30–31.

6 Wright, 30. Walton argues that "children's games serve purposes far more significant than that of keeping them happy and out of mischief. It is generally recognized, I believe, that such games—and imaginative activities generally—do indeed, as their prevalence suggests, have a profound role in our efforts to cope with our environment. Children in the Auschwitz concentration camp played a game called 'going to the gas chamber.' . . . In 'playing' it they were, I suspect, facing the reality of genocide with the utmost seriousness." Walton, *Mimesis as Make-Believe*, 12.

7 Bedford, "Gross Sales." Andy Warhol, Peter Max, and Oscar de la Renta are among the famous figures inspired by Barbie. Her

greatest appeal to children is among girls in North America. She inspires adults and children alike to act out their dreams.

8 The most recent figures show that Barbie has occupied more than two hundred professions. See Bedford.

9 Mattel's marketing strategy involves clever, context-sensitive back-stories aimed at drawing in new buyers and sustaining interest in Barbie products. For a fascinating look at Barbie's complex meanings, see Jacqueline Urla and Alan C. Swedlund, "The Anthropometry of Barbie: Unsettling Ideals of the Feminine Body in Popular Culture," in *Feminism and the Body*, ed. Londa Schiebinger (Oxford: Oxford University Press, 2000), 398, 406. One example of a backstory designed to increase sales is a CNNMoney article from 2011: *Ken and Barbie broke up to spend quality time apart. He wooed her back over Valentine's Day.* Parija Kavilanz, "Barbie and Ken: Back Together on Valentine's Day," CNNMoney, February 14, 2011, https://tinyurl.com/kdhwhetz.

10 The ideal woman produced by the archetypal performances of Mary, Athena, Venus, and Barbie is a womb and a cradle, a vessel and a guard, a lover and a patron, and a muse and a prize. In sum, the ideal woman is an alluring material site for male psychic retreat from the masculine world.

11 Urla and Swedlund argue that the fantasy or "dream" of Barbie rests on "leisure and consumption, not production" ("Anthropometry of Barbie," 404).

12 Judith Butler and Liz Kotz, "The Body You Want: Liz Kotz Interviews Judith Butler," *Artforum* 31, no. 3 (November 1992): 85–86. This interview takes place between the publication of *Gender Trouble* and *Bodies That Matter*. Butler's lucid responses clarify some of the misconceptions of her view of gender as performativity and expand upon her appropriation of citationality, among other critical concepts.

13 Butler conceives of gender as a function of reiterative performances of signs that signify "woman," coordinate female identity, and normalize female behaviors. In her Kotz interview in *Artforum*, Butler maintains that "gender is a kind of psychic norm and cultural practice" that will, therefore, "always elude a fixed definition" (Butler and Kotz, "Body You Want," 86).

14 Woman is defined as a nonthinking, reproductive object and an opposing force to man, defined in terms of mind as a thinking,

productive subject who is naturally designed and situated in the masculine order to dominate, use, and regard woman as subordinate.

15 Judith Butler, *Gender Trouble: Feminism and the Subversion of Identity* (New York: Routledge, 1990), 33. Butler defines gender specifically as "the repeated stylization of the body" (33). Hence she does not eschew materiality or substance entirely, as she is sometimes accused of doing. The body is not erased or invisible.

16 Judith Butler, *Bodies That Matter: On the Discursive Limits of "Sex"* (New York: Routledge, 2011), 36.

17 I make this argument in J. Lenore Wright, "Relationality and Life: Phenomenological Reflections on Miscarriage," *International Journal of Feminist Approaches to Bioethics* 11, no. 2 (Fall 2018): 135–56.

18 Butler and Kotz, "Body You Want," 84.

19 Regarding the concept of "female subjectivity," if personal identities are formed and embodied in differently sexed, gendered, racialized, aged, weighted, and abled bodies, then traditional phenomenological accounts of "the subject" cannot explain embodied existence fully. Phenomenologists must, therefore, expand their descriptions of being human—descriptions of bodily situated and historically informed personhood—to include descriptions of distinctive, singular, embodied perceptions and experiences. The growing awareness and individual articulation of gender identity to include both nonconforming and transgender identities moves in this direction. Beauvoir's descriptions of women's embodiment in her autobiographical, literary, and philosophical texts constitute a helpful model of what a refined, feminist-informed phenomenology might look like. Following Beauvoir's lead, we must learn to speak the experiences we live and perceive rather than the experiences we theorize as reflective of (or normative of) human forms of life. Women especially benefit from a philosophical tradition that values phenomenologically informed perspectives. Working alongside Jean-Paul Sartre, Beauvoir affirms the centrality phenomenology gives to experience, a centrality that reflects her dual existentialist and feminist commitments. "It is not necessary to *think* a situation to *exist* it," she writes in volume 2 of *The Second Sex*, titled "Lived Experience" (294). Beauvoir's engagement with phenomenology is tightly linked to her commitment to sexual difference. Like traditional phenomenologists, she regards humans

as "situated beings" who are "always involved in the world, and so can only be understood within the total, very complex context of that world" and "as beings who continually give meaning to their situation." Karen Vintges, "*The Second Sex* and Philosophy," in *Feminist Interpretations of Simone de Beauvoir*, ed. Margaret A. Simons (University Park: Pennsylvania State University Press, 1995), 46. She departs from traditional phenomenology, however, by investigating human relations with others and how these relations shape modes of perception and the formation of personal identity, particularly gender identity. Feminist philosophers share Beauvoir's interest in the processes that constitute women's perceptions, experiences, and identities. Some aim to describe the processes that generate specific forms of life within which women find themselves while others seek to alter the processes that limit women's freedom in the world and, thus, alter the specific forms of life women embody. For Beauvoir, understanding the biological, social, and cultural processes that constitute "woman"—biological, social, and cultural forces that produce gendered individuals—is first and foremost a phenomenological, rather than political, task because individuals "[cast]" themselves "into the world" not with a set of "ready-made qualities" or "brute fact[s]" but as "object[s] of sympathy or repulsion." Simone de Beauvoir, *The Ethics of Ambiguity*, trans. Bernard Frechtman (New York: Philosophical Library, 1948), 41. Beauvoir is especially critical of the ways in which a woman's body and the functions it is considered destined to perform have confined women to a preassigned essence and identity: woman is a womb. Beauvoir's critique of womanhood—"One is not born, but rather becomes, a woman"—is informed by her understanding of human subjects as beings-in-relation-to-others (Beauvoir, *Second Sex*, 293).

Appropriating Merleau-Ponty's notion of self as body-subject, a subject that inheres with material bodies and stands in relation to other body-subjects (a foil to Hegel's displaced and abstract individual who is always surpassing mutually recognized individuals), Beauvoir defines human subjects as *bodies-in-relation* to others. Subjects—not "a subject" or "the subject" but distinctive, singular, differently embodied subjects—are encountered by oneself and others as a given, and they are also realized as living, operative standpoints from which embodied existence is defined and experienced. Her view of subjectivity as intersubjectivity assumes a rich, relational account of personhood.

20 Wright, "Wonder of Barbie," 32.

21 Wright, 32–33. Insofar as Barbie allows representation of cultural icons to be open and unmandated, Barbie encourages a creative interpretation of identity and image construction.

22 The religious function of dolls aligns Barbie with Mary, Athena, and Venus's spiritual significations.

23 The New York artist Laurie Simmons incorporated Love Dolls into her photographic work. See Anne Bothwell, "Laurie Simmons Explores Memory and Domesticity with Dolls," Art&Seek, October 15, 2018, https://tinyurl.com/5h7ht4vk.

24 Barbie is neither a sex doll nor a Marian, salvific figure. She follows Athena into the male world but fails to signify woman as thinker and leader. She exemplifies the physical perfection of Venus but avoids her important cultural signification. Barbie is nevertheless embedded in the same narratological myth of Mary, Athena, and Venus and performs a similar archetypal function: *she gives the world order and beauty.* Mary, Athena, and Venus produce order and beauty through childbearing, nation building, and relational bonding, respectively. Barbie, by contrast, does not *produce* order and beauty; rather, she suggests their production by selling images of order and beauty.

25 In Barbie's case, she erupts from the head of Ruth Handler rather than the head of Zeus.

26 Barbie is, technically speaking, designed rather than born. Unlike Mary, Athena, and Venus, she poses no threat to the male world. She bears no unusual relationship to obvious father figures (her lack of divine affiliation neutralizes her potential subversion). She signifies a traditional narrative of feminine reproductivity. A woman (metaphorically) births her. She in turn inspires the imaginations and creative visions of others. She hails from Wisconsin, a wholesome midwestern state. She embodies the professional aspirations and progressive power of women of her era in a (literally) contained and attractive package. Barbie reads as safe. Like Mary, Athena, and Venus, Barbie belongs to a lineage of female archetypes who codify female agency and identity. Although she is a manufactured archetype—not a woman like Mary or a goddess like Athena and Venus—her ontological status is irrelevant for understanding

her archetypal import. In fact, her toy status heightens the need for feminist critiques of women's subjectivity because of the implicit claim that women are, like Barbie, playthings in men's games of make-believe.

27 If Barbie's projected wealth rather than the embodied work of Mary, Athena, and Venus can protect humanity from the chaos and ugliness of moral sin, political disorder, and social discord, then the path to salvation is clear—and, at least for a few, attainable. (Money can, with apologies to Annie Lennox, buy it. And "it" refers to everything in the Barbie world.)

28 Urla and Swedlund observe that while Barbie's identity is mutable, "*her hyper-slender, big-chested body has remained fundamentally unchanged over the years*" ("Anthropometry of Barbie," 407 [italics in original]).

29 Mary is the medium through which the Hebraic narrative of a future messiah is acted out. The story fails without her. But she is not the story. God's desire to save creation through the birth of Mary's son is the main act.

30 If, as Urla and Swedlund argue, Barbie is a meaning system in itself, there is support for Barbie's subversion of femininity: "Hers is a body of hard edges, distinct borders, self-control. . . . Barbie's body may signify for women the pleasure of control and mastery, both of which are highly valued traits in American society and predominantly associated with masculinity" ("Anthropometry of Barbie," 420).

31 Barbie's measurements, posture, and proportions have not been changed significantly in fifty-five years (Urla and Swedlund, 407).

32 "Barbie has had such wide influence on American fashion and culture," remarks Steven Kolb, president and CEO of the CFDA. "Her story personally resonates with so many CFDA members that the Board of Directors decided to honor her with the special tribute." In fact, fellow 2019 CFDA honoree Bob Mackie, who is being celebrated with the Geoffrey Beene Lifetime Achievement Award this year, collaborated with Barbie on a collector doll in 1990. "It is a tremendous honor for Barbie to be recognized by the CFDA Board of Directors for her contributions to American fashion. For the past six decades, Barbie has inspired and been inspired by fashion and creative communities," Richard Dickson, Mattel's president and chief operating officer, said in a statement. "Barbie has had the great privilege of collaborating with some of the greatest designer [*sic*] of our time

and this award is a moment to celebrate her lasting influence." Marc Karimzadeh, "Barbie to Receive Board of Directors' Special Tribute," CFDA, May 16, 2019, https://tinyurl.com/42k67vcm.

33 Though important ethical and ontological questions also arise out of the image-making endeavors of toy makers, advertisers, and television producers, I set aside these questions in this book. I focus instead on popular culture. To be sure, popular cultural icons have had a profound effect on the American psyche, particularly in the shaping of our views of beauty and gender. Though philosophers may understandably disdain pop culture—a domain of experience that feeds upon transitory values and trends—none will deny the powerful effect pop culture and television have on the American mind. The philosophical and cultural analysis I offer here responds to this fact.

34 Barbie's iconic status reflects "late capitalist constructions of femininity" by pairing her "consumption with the achievement of femininity" and the "appropriately gendered body" (Urla and Swedlund, "Anthropometry of Barbie," 401).

35 Urla and Swedlund, 405.

36 In Urla and Swedlund's words, Barbie "is always a perfect fit, always able to consume and be consumed" (424).

37 Barbie's popularity within gay culture is well established: "It is Barbie, with her molded-by-Mattel body, who stands in for the drag queen, commanding the spectator, whip in hand, to *work her body*. Barbie, in this fantasy-scape, becomes the mistress of body discipline, exposing simultaneously the artifice of gender and the feminine body" (Urla and Swedlund, 422). Barbie is arguably the most real and relevant archetype of the female subject because of her ubiquitous, mimetic presence. People everywhere want to play Barbie: female, male, straight, queer, cisgender, transgender, nonbinary/nonconforming, and others. Barbie is equally admired in heteronormative and LGBTQIA+ communities.

38 Feminist aestheticians owe a debt of gratitude to Annelies Hofmeyr for her reproduction of classical Barbie as "Trophy Wife Barbie." Hofmeyr's background in graphic design and jewelry making elevates her satirical presentation of Barbie's dream world, complete with pink guns, binge drinking, and sagging skin. Susannah Breslin's interview with Hofmeyr in *Forbes* magazine. Annelies Hofmeyr, "Meet Trophy Wife Barbie: She Smokes, Drinks, and Raises Hell," interview by Susannah Breslin, *Forbes*, June 1, 2016, https://tinyurl.com/mcv4fxkv.

39 Trophy Wife Barbie (@trophywifebarbie), Instagram, https://www
.instagram.com/trophywifebarbie/. Trophy Wife Barbie is often
featured with her transgender friend, Kendra, who is undergoing
hormone replacement therapy.

40 Sarah Williamson, "Meet ArtActivistBarbie, the Fearless Funny
Feminist Taking on a White Male Art World," MuseumNext,
May 18, 2020, https://tinyurl.com/4f6jzkka.

41 Heidi Bostic, "Literary Women, Reason, and the Fiction of Enlightenment," *French Review* 85, no. 6 (May 2012): 1024–1038.
Bostic draws upon the art activist group Guerrilla Girls.

42 Luce Irigaray, *This Sex Which Is Not One*, trans. Catherine Porter
(Ithaca, NY: Cornell University Press, 1985), 26.

Conclusion

1 Virginia Woolf, *A Room of One's Own* (New York: Harcourt, Brace,
1929), 110–11.

2 The second-century church father Clement of Alexandria argues
that every woman should experience shame at the thought that she
is a woman. "Statements on Women by Church Fathers, Doctors,
and Saints: Clement of Alexandria, Pedagogues II, 33, 2," Theology Library, Spring Hill College, accessed May 24, 2021, http://
theolibrary.shc.edu/resources/women.htm.

3 For these and other theological perspectives on women, go to Hope
Abigail Freeman, "The Truth of the Church's History," in *Understanding Biblical Gender Equality: Women and Men in Marriage,
the Home, and the Church, Walk in Truth* (blog), accessed May 24,
2021, https://tinyurl.com/efckdcx7.

4 Joanna Ebenstein, *The Anatomical Venus* (London: Thames &
Hudson, 2016), 19.

5 Straight, cisgender dads can perform "motherly" childcare duties
without fearing a loss of male authority if these duties no longer hold
a female signification—that is, if soothing, feeding, and nurturing
children is not a female-exclusive or feminine-coded activity. Similarly, transgender parents can care for their children without compromising their gender identities if childcare duties lose their gendered
(male and female) significations. In this way, heterosexual, cisgender
men can come to appreciate the plight of transgender parents.

6 Woolf, *Room of One's Own.*

7 Woolf, 199.

Bibliography

Apollodorus. *Apollodorus'* Library *and Hyginus'* Fabulae*: Two Handbooks of Greek Mythology*. Translated by R. Scott Smith and Stephen M. Trzaskoma. Indianapolis, IN: Hackett, 2007.

Arendt, Hannah. *The Human Condition*. 2nd ed. Chicago: University of Chicago Press, 1998.

Aristophanes. *Lysistrata*. Translated by Dudley Fitts. New York: Harcourt, Brace, 1954.

Augustine. *Confessions*. Translated by Henry Chadwick. Oxford: Oxford University Press, 1998.

Bartky, Sandra Lee. "Foucault, Femininity, and the Modernization of Patriarchal Power." In *Feminist Theory Reader: Local and Global Perspectives*, 4th ed., edited by Carole R. McCann and Seung-Kyung Kim, 466–480. New York: Routledge, 2017.

Bean, Kellie. *Post-backlash Feminism: Women and the Media since Reagan-Bush*. Jefferson, NC: McFarland, 2007.

Beauvoir, Simone de. *The Ethics of Ambiguity*. Translated by Bernard Frechtman. New York: Philosophical Library, 1948.

———. *The Second Sex*. Translated by Constance Borde and Sheila Malovany-Chevallier. London: Jonathan Cape, 2009.

Bedford, Emma. "Gross Sales of Mattel's Barbie Brand Worldwide from 2012 to 2019 (in Millions of U.S. Dollars)." Statista. March 5, 2020. https://tinyurl.com/vwmfn9w7.

Bordo, Susan. "Feminism, Foucault and the Politics of the Body." In *Feminist Theory and the Body: A Reader*, edited by Janet Price and Margrit Shildrick, 246–257. New York: Routledge, 2010.

———. "The Empire of Images in Our World of Bodies." *The Chronicle of Higher Education*. December 19, 2003. https://tinyurl.com/3jvwkx8h.

Bostic, Heidi. "Literary Women, Reason, and the Fiction of Enlightenment." *French Review* 85, no. 6 (May 2012): 1024–1038.

Bothwell, Anne. "Laurie Simmons Explores Memory and Domesticity with Dolls." Art&Seek. October 15, 2018. https://tinyurl.com/5h7ht4vk.

Botticelli, Sandro. *Birth of Venus*. Ca. 1485. Tempera on canvas. Le Gallerie Degli Uffizi, Florence, Italy. https://www.uffizi.it/en/artworks/birth-of-venus.

Brown, Rachel Fulton. "Mary in the Scriptures." In *Advancing Mariology: The Theotokos Lectures 2008–2017*, edited by Jame Schaefer, 205–234. Marquette Studies in Theology 89. Milwaukee, WI: Marquette University Press, 2017.

Butler, Judith. *Bodies That Matter: On the Discursive Limits of "Sex."* New York: Routledge, 2011.

———. *Gender Trouble: Feminism and the Subversion of Identity*. New York: Routledge, 1990.

Butler, Judith, and Liz Kotz. "The Body You Want: Liz Kotz Interviews Judith Butler." *Artforum* 31, no. 3 (November 1992): 82–89.

Coffin, Judith G. *Sex, Love, and Letters: Writing Simone de Beauvoir*. Ithaca, NY: Cornell University Press, 2020.

Connelly, Joan Breton. *Portrait of a Priestess: Women and Ritual in Ancient Greece*. Princeton, NJ: Princeton University Press, 2007.

Diprose, Rosalyn. *The Bodies of Women: Ethics, Embodiment and Sexual Difference*. London: Routledge, 1994.

Duncan, Byard. "Dr. Laura Schlessinger." Generation Progress. Center for American Progress. September 9, 2010. https://genprogress.org/dr-laura-schlessinger/.

Dworkin, Andrea. *Intercourse*. 20th anniversary ed. New York: Basic Books, 2007.

Ebenstein, Joanna. *The Anatomical Venus*. London: Thames & Hudson, 2016.

Encyclopaedia Britannica Online. s.v. "Our Lady of Guadalupe." Last modified May 15, 2020. https://tinyurl.com/9sfu9yvs.

Fausto-Sterling, Anne. "Menopause: The Storm before the Calm." In *Feminist Theory and the Body: A Reader*, edited by Janet Price and Margrit Shildrick, 169–178. New York: Routledge, 2010.

Fiore, Julia. "Why Jesus and Mary Always Wear Red and Blue in Art History." Artsy. December 19, 2018. https://tinyurl.com/dm8t4ajr.

Fletcher, Elizabeth. "Mary in Nazareth—the Real Woman." Women in the Bible. 2006. https://tinyurl.com/bhw9u82s.

Friedan, Betty. *The Feminine Mystique*. New York: W. W. Norton, 1963.

Gambero, Luigi. *Mary and the Fathers of the Church: The Blessed Virgin Mary in Patristic Thought*. Translated by Thomas Buffer. San Francisco: Ignatius, 1999.

Gatens, Moira. "Beauvoir and Biology: A Second Look." In *The Cambridge Companion to Simone de Beauvoir*, edited by Claudia Card, 266–285. Cambridge: Cambridge University Press, 2006.

———. *Imaginary Bodies: Ethics, Power and Corporeality*. London: Routledge, 1996.

Gaventa, Beverly Roberts. *Mary: Glimpses of the Mother of Jesus*. Columbia: University of South Carolina Press, 1995.

Gibson, David. "Christmas' Missing Icon: Mary Breastfeeding Jesus." *Washington Post*, December 10, 2012. https://tinyurl.com/ah7zmfm.

Grosz, Elizabeth A. *Space, Time, and Perversion: Essays on the Politics of Bodies*. London: Routledge, 1995.

———. *Volatile Bodies: Toward a Corporeal Feminism*. Bloomington: Indiana University Press, 1994.

Guenther, Lisa. *The Gift of the Other: Levinas and the Politics of Reproduction*. Albany: State University of New York Press, 2006.

Halberstam, Jack. *Trans*: A Quick and Quirky Account of Gender Variability*. Oakland: University of California Press, 2018.

Hofmeyr, Annelies. "Meet Trophy Wife Barbie: She Smokes, Drinks, and Raises Hell." By Susannah Breslin. *Forbes*, June 1, 2016. https://tinyurl.com/mcv4fxkv.

Irigaray, Luce. *This Sex Which Is Not One*. Translated by Catherine Porter. Ithaca, NY: Cornell University Press, 1985.

Johnson, Elizabeth A. "The Mighty from Their Thrones." In *Advancing Mariology: The Theotokos Lectures 2008–2017*, edited by Jame Schaefer, 235–256. Marquette Studies in Theology 89. Milwaukee, WI: Marquette University Press, 2017.

Kamitsuka, Margaret D. *Abortion and the Christian Tradition: A Pro-Choice Theological Ethic*. Louisville, KY: Westminster John Knox, 2019.

Karimzadeh, Marc. "Barbie to Receive Board of Directors' Special Tribute." CFDA. May 16, 2019. https://tinyurl.com/42k67vcm.

Kavilanz, Parija. "Barbie and Ken: Back Together on Valentine's Day." CNNMoney, February 14, 2011. https://tinyurl.com/kdhwhetz.

Klaver, Elizabeth. *Sites of Autopsy in Contemporary Culture*. Albany: State University of New York Press, 2005.

Laqueur, Thomas. *Making Sex: Body and Gender from the Greeks to Freud*. Cambridge, MA: Harvard University Press, 1994.

Llywelyn, Dorian. "Mirror of Justice, Mother of Mercy." In *Advancing Mariology: The Theotokos Lectures 2008–2017*, edited by Jame Schaefer, 283–314. Marquette Studies in Theology 89. Milwaukee, WI: Marquette University Press, 2017.

Loraux, Nicole. *The Children of Athena: Athenian Ideas about Citizenship and the Division between the Sexes*. Translated by Caroline Levine. Princeton, NJ: Princeton University Press, 1993.

Lorde, Audre. "The Master's Tools Will Never Dismantle the Master's House." In *Sister Outsider*, 110–113. Trumansburg, NY: Crossing, 1984.

Macrone, Michael. *Brush Up Your Mythology!* New York: Gramercy, 1999.

Marshall, Helen. "Our Bodies, Ourselves: Why We Should Add Old Fashioned Empirical Phenomenology to the New Theories of the Body." In *Feminist Theory and the Body: A Reader*, edited by Janet Price and Margrit Shildrick, 64–75. New York: Routledge, 2010.

Martin, Emily. "The Egg and the Sperm: How Science Has Constructed a Romance Based on Stereotypical Male-Female Roles." In *Feminist Theory and the Body: A Reader*, edited by Janet Price and Margrit Shildrick, 179–189. New York: Routledge, 1999.

Mayerson, Philip. *Classical Mythology in Literature, Art, and Music.* Newburyport, MA: Focus, 2001.

Miles, Margaret R. *A Complex Delight: The Secularization of the Breast, 1350–1750.* Berkeley: University of California Press, 2008.

Moffett, Chris. "About." *Splitting Skulls* (blog). Columbia University. March 26, 2010. https://blogs.cuit.columbia.edu/cm2189/tag/zeus/.

Mullin, Amy. *Reconceiving Pregnancy and Childcare: Ethics, Experience, and Reproductive Labor.* Cambridge: Cambridge University Press, 2005.

Mulvey, Laura. "Visual Pleasure and Narrative Cinema." In *Visual and Other Pleasures*, 14–26. Bloomington: Indiana University Press, 1989.

Murphy, Francesca Aran. "Mary as 'Omnipotent by Grace.'" In *Advancing Mariology: The Theotokos Lectures 2008–2017*, edited by Jame Schaefer, 179–204. Marquette Studies in Theology 89. Milwaukee, WI: Marquette University Press, 2017.

Nietzsche, Friedrich. "Thus Spoke Zarathustra." In *The Portable Nietzsche*, translated by Walter Kaufmann, 103–439. New York: Penguin, 1954.

Oliver, Kelly. *Knock Me Up, Knock Me Down: Images of Pregnancy in Hollywood Films.* New York: Columbia University Press, 2012.

"Our History." About Barbie. Barbie.mattel.com. Accessed November 26, 2020. https://tinyurl.com/4ejcjsju.

Paris, Ginette. *Pagan Meditations: The Worlds of Aphrodite, Artemis, and Hestia.* Translated by Gwendolyn Moore. Dallas: Spring, 1987.

Paul VI. *Marialis Cultus: For the Right Ordering and Development of Devotion to the Blessed Virgin Mary.* Holy See. February 2, 1974. https://tinyurl.com/nkahwdua.

Pelikan, Jaroslav. *Mary through the Centuries: Her Place in the History of Culture.* New Haven, CT: Yale University Press, 1996.

Pelikan, Jaroslav, David Flusser, and Justin Lang. *Mary: Images of the Mother of Jesus in Jewish and Christian Perspective.* Minneapolis: Fortress, 2005.

Persaud, T. V. N., Marios Loukas, and R. Shane Tubbs. *A History of Human Anatomy.* 2nd ed. Springfield, IL: Charles C. Thomas, 2014.

Petherbridge, Deanna, and Ludmilla Jordanova. *The Quick and the Dead: Artists and Anatomy.* Berkeley: University of California Press, 1997.

Pompeian Connections: Networks in Pompeii and the Roman World (blog). https://pompeiinetworks.wordpress.com/page/4/.

Pooler, David K., and Amanda Frey. "Responding to Survivors of Clergy Sexual Abuse." In *Treating Trauma in Christian Counseling*, edited by Heather Davediuk Gingrich and Fred C. Gingrich, 188–210. Downers Grove, IL: InterVarsity, 2017.

Price, Janet, and Margrit Shildrick, eds. *Feminist Theory and the Body: A Reader*. New York: Routledge, 1999.

Realy, Margaret Rose. "Walnuts, Thanksgiving, and a Garden Catechism." Patheos. November 14, 2014. https://tinyurl.com/2yvmxjkh.

Rubin, Miri. *Mother of God: A History of the Virgin Mary*. New Haven, CT: Yale University Press, 2009.

Schaberg, Jane. *The Illegitimacy of Jesus: A Feminist Theological Interpretation of the Infancy Narratives*. San Francisco: Harper & Row, 1987.

Schaefer, Jame, ed. *Advancing Mariology: The Theotokos Lectures 2008–2017*. Marquette Studies in Theology 89. Milwaukee, WI: Marquette University Press, 2017.

Schiebinger, Londa. *Nature's Body: Gender in the Making of Modern Science*. New Brunswick, NJ: Rutgers University Press, 2010.

Schlessinger, Laura, ed. *Dr. Laura* (blog). Dr. Laura website. https://family.drlaura.com/blog?categoryID=1

Schultz, Anne-Marie. *Plato's Socrates as Narrator: A Philosophical Muse*. Lanham, MD: Lexington Books, 2013.

———. *Plato's Socrates on Socrates: Socratic Self-Disclosure and the Public Practice of Philosophy*. Lanham, MD: Lexington Books, 2020.

Seyffert, Oskar. *A Dictionary of Classical Antiquities*. Edited by Henry Nettleship and J. E. Sandys. New York: Meridian, 1956.

Southern Baptist Convention. "The Baptist Faith and Message." September 1, 2016. https://tinyurl.com/mfpu6bsw.

"Statements on Women by Church Fathers, Doctors, and Saints: Clement of Alexandria, Pedagogues II, 33, 2." Theology Library. Spring Hill College. Accessed May 24, 2021. http://theolibrary.shc.edu/resources/women.htm.

"The Queen's Four Maries." Scots Language Centre. Centre for the Scots Leid. Accessed August 18, 2020. https://www.scotslanguage.com/articles/node/id/436.

Trophy Wife Barbie (@trophywifebarbie). Instagram. https://www
.instagram.com/trophywifebarbie/.

Tucker, Jason. "#Blessed: What Jesus Really Says about It." *Jason
Tucker* (blog). February 18, 2019. https://www.jasontucker.faith/
blessed/.

*Understanding Biblical Gender Equality: Women and Men in Marriage,
the Home, and the Church, Walk in Truth* (blog). https://tinyurl
.com/efckdcx7.

Urla, Jacqueline, and Alan C. Swedlund. "The Anthropometry of
Barbie: Unsettling Ideals of the Feminine Body in Popular
Culture." In *Feminism and the Body*, edited by Londa Schiebinger,
397–428. Oxford: Oxford University Press, 2000.

Vintges, Karen. "*The Second Sex* and Philosophy." In *Feminist
Interpretations of Simone de Beauvoir*, edited by Margaret A.
Simons, 45–58. University Park: Pennsylvania State University
Press, 1995.

Walton, Kendall L. *Mimesis as Make-Believe: On the Foundations of the
Representational Arts*. Cambridge, MA: Harvard University Press,
1990.

Wendell, Susan. "Feminism, Disability, and Transcendence of the Body."
In *Feminist Theory and the Body: A Reader*, edited by Janet Price and
Margrit Shildrick, 324–334. New York: Routledge, 2010.

Williams, Florence. *Breasts: A Natural and Unnatural History*. New
York: W. W. Norton, 2012.

Williamson, Sarah. "Meet ArtActivistBarbie, the Fearless Funny
Feminist Taking on a White Male Art World." MuseumNext.
May 18, 2020. https://tinyurl.com/4f6jzkka.

Wollstonecraft, Mary. *A Vindication of the Rights of Woman: With
Strictures on Political and Moral Subjects*. Edited by D. L.
Macdonald and Kathleen Scherf. Peterborough, ON: Broadview,
1997.

Woolf, Virginia. *A Room of One's Own*. New York: Harcourt,
Brace, 1929.

Wright, J. Lenore. "Relationality and Life: Phenomenological
Reflections on Miscarriage." *International Journal of Feminist
Approaches to Bioethics* 11, no. 2 (Fall 2018): 135–156.

———. "The Wonder of Barbie: Popular Culture and the
Making of Female Identity." *Essays in Philosophy* 4, no. 1
(January 2003): 28–52.

Index

abortion, 14, 18, 62, 146n30, 152–53n74

Abrahamic, 16, 21–22

abstinence, 17, 145n24

Acropolis, 44

Adam, 23

Aeneas, 69, 127

aesthetic: allure, 80; forces, 134; imagination of artists, 77; pleasure, 13, 60; trend, 64

aesthetics, 67, 84

agency, 86, 109; novel forms of, 44

Alan (Barbie doll), 131

American dream, 95

anatomical: atlases, 64, 160n76; claims, 100; contexts, 166n35; definitions, 5; discourse, 87; dolls, 86; drawings, 26, 160n76; model, 86, 89; paintings, 125; science, 85; structures, 1, 85; study, 3, 64

Anatomical Venus, 86–88, 167n41, 167n47

anatomy, 13, 84–85, 159n53, 168n55

Aphrodite, 58–59, 68, 160–61n2, 161n4, 161n7, 163n15

Apollodorus, 38, 153–54n2, 155n15

archetypes, and agency, ix

Arendt, Hannah, 46–47, 65, 157nn33–35, 160n78

Aristophanes, 44, 156n25

ArtActivistBarbie, 116–17, 177n40

Arterbury, Andrew, xii, 145n24, 146n36, 152n74

assisted reproductive technology (ART), 135, 142n7, 145n25

Athena: and agency, 65; as archetype, 6, 60, 65, 137, 142n9, 157n30, 161n10, 171n10; and Barbie, 131–32, 174nn24–27; beauty contest, participation in, 58; birth of, 38–39, 54, 153n2, 163n18; and birth of ideas, 134; and birth of the polis, 53; and birth of political structures, 75; and birth of political valor, 49; and birth of politics, 40; and birth of the state, 127; celebration in honor of, 158n37; and civic engagement, 56; and civic order, 127; contrast with Aphrodite, 163n15; dutiful refusal of marriage, 59; engendering civic order, 96; Euripides's reference to, 159n52; and female agency, 133; and female subjectivity, repression of, 66; and feminine order, repression of the, 47; and feminism, 61–62, 66; as goddess, 34, 36, 59; as goddess without a mother, 159n52; intellectual prowess of, 68; and Mary, 9, 63–64, 75, 90; masculine norms, appropriation of, 43; as metaphoric mother, 69, 98; as nonsexual, 45; overseeing birth of Pandora, 153n1; and performance of motherhood, 60, 83, 91, 98, 127; physical strength of, 43, 52; and the polis, 36, 47, 53, 59–60, 74, 163n21; and political authority, 36, 44; power of, 104–5; and pregnancy, 34, 37, 45, 49, 88; as rational, 43, 45, 70; reality and, 61, 127; relationship to the masculine, 39–43, 47, 50, 53–55, 76, 105, 133, 154n10, 157n36; rule through mental acumen, 52; sexual desire, repression of, 36; strength of, 102; and Venus, 68–70, 73, 90; virginity of, 35, 57; as warrior, 47–51, 74; as warrior-goddess, 74; and wisdom, 43; as wisdom, personification of, 35–36; as woman-goddess, 35, 37, 50, 52, 126; and womanhood, 41, 154–55n11; and womb, 5, 44, 56, 59, 61; and womb as political space, 34, 36, 126

Athens, 45, 49, 53, 59, 153n1, 154n4, 156n26

Augustine, Saint, 146n29
Augustinian tradition, 149n52
authority, ix, 1, 86, 137,
    157n30
autonomy, 7, 25, 42, 71,
    104–5

babies, 19, 32, 57, 94, 98, 136,
    168n67
Barbie: and agency, 98–99; and
    American femininity, 105;
    as archetype, 137, 161n10,
    171n10, 174n26; as artistic
    medium, 110–17; and Ath-
    ena, 37; and authority, 99;
    avoidance of motherhood,
    98; and Beyoncé, 112–14;
    and birth identity, 114; and
    birth identity, surrendering
    of, 106–7; body of, 175n28,
    175nn30–31; as brand, 94,
    109, 170n4, 170–71n7,
    171nn8–9; and civic order,
    132; coding herself as Bar-
    bie, 112; commodified fem-
    ininity of, 110, 118, 129; as
    a consumer brand, 103; and
    consumer desires, 97, 129;
    creation of, 94, 174n26;
    cultural power of, 95; doll,
    93, 95, 97, 108–9, 112,
    116, 174n22, 174n24; doll,
    as religious symbol, 103;
    Dream House, 94; dream of,
    171n11; and female agency,
    118; and female normativity,
    96; feminine identity of,
    95–98, 107; and feminine
    norms, 107, 110; femininity,
    normative representation
    of, 97; and feminism, 101;
    gay culture, popularity in,
    175n37; gender performa-
    tivity of, 99, 102, 171n12;
    heteronormative commu-
    nities, admired in, 176n37;
    influence of, 175–76n32;
    and Kylie Jenner, 111–12;
    and Mary, 104–5; narrated
    history of, 103; norms asso-
    ciated with, 116; ontological
    status of, 174n26; opinions
    of, 93; as other directed, 96;
    performance of femininity,
    99, 131; performativity of,
    114; as postmodern critic,
    131; and pregnancy, 95–96,
    118, 129, 131–32; and real-
    ity, 105, 129; as role model,
    93; and RuPaul, 114–15;
    social norms, influence over,
    111; as teacher, 96; as toy,
    94, 98–99, 103–7, 116,
    169n1, 170n2, 174–75n26;
    wealth of, 175n27; as
    woman, 104; and womb, 5,
    9, 95, 103, 134; and womb
    as figurative space, 129
Barker, Margaret, 144n17
Bartky, Sandra Lee, 147n40,
    151n67, 165n34
Bean, Kellie, 167n42
Beaton, Mary, 8, 140n4
Beauvoir, Simone de, ix, 9, 46,
    54, 80, 101, 123, 135, 137,
    140n2, 140n8, 148n50,
    154n9, 157n32, 159n55,
    164n28, 172–73n19

Bedford, Emma, 170n4, 170n7, 171n8
Benedict XVI (pope), 23
Berkeley, Busby, 165n33
Beyoncé, 30–32, 112–13
biblical: exhortation, 145n25; information, 16; presentation, 145n36; scholars, 144n17; text, 146n30; views, 26
biblical mandate, 21
binary, 17; construction of Descartes's, 54; male-female, 47, 59, 154n10; Mary-Athena, 75, 90; sex attributions, 99; sexual, 42
birth: of Aphrodite, 161n2; of Athena, 38–39, 54; of babies, 19; biological, 65; of a child, 88; of divine savior, 63; of Jesus, 19; of Mary's son, 175n29; of Pandora, 153n1; as unwombed activity, 37; of Venus, 71, 73
birth control, 62
Birth of Venus, 77, 161n3
#blessed, 32, 153n75
Bordo, Susan, 147n40, 158n40
Bostic, Heidi, xi, 158n38, 177n41
Bothwell, Anne, 174n23
Botticelli, Sandro, 77, 161n3
Bozon, Michel, 165n30
breasts, 26, 27, 52, 63, 72, 81, 87, 98, 101, 150n58, 151n64, 163n17, 165n35
Brown, Rachel Fulton, 143nn11–12, 144nn17–20

Burgon vase, 48, 158n37
Butler, Judith, 99–100, 102, 171nn12–13, 172nn15–18

Caelus (Uranus or Ouranos), 68, 72, 81, 90
Caesar, Julius, 69
career, 56, 66, 92, 98, 103, 157n30
Carmichael, Mary, 8, 139–40n4
Cartesian: mind-body dualism, 59, 99–100; philosophy, 54
celibate, 17, 36, 126
chaste, 17, 19–20, 70, 83, 151n58
chastity, 14, 17, 22, 69, 91, 146n29
child, infant, 26
childbearing, 7, 22, 40, 51, 54, 56, 97, 174n24
childbirth, x, 8, 20, 27, 76, 122, 133
Christ, 23, 26, 29, 63
Christ child, 28–29, 150n58
Christian theology, 16
church, 16, 19–21, 24, 26, 30, 63, 141n4, 149n52, 152n51, 152n73, 165n35
church fathers, 146n30
citizenship, 44, 53, 153n1
civic: activities, 71; ideals, 36; ideas, 37; imagination, 39, 157n30; leader, 37; leadership, 37, 43, 133; life, 2, 39, 65–66; order, 36, 48; structures, 70
civilization, 43, 66, 73
Clarkson, Craig, xiii, 152n74
Clement of Alexandria, 177n2

Clinton, Hillary, 45, 157n30
coding: of embodied female activities, 60; masculine-gendered, 52; of parental activities, 76, 133; sacred, of sex, 83; of womb, 68; womb as sacred, 14, 125
Coffin, Judith G, 157n32, 165nn30–32
Concordia (Harmonia), 70
Connelly, Joan Breton, 154nn4–6, 154n9, 154–55n11, 156nn23–24, 156n27, 157n36, 159nn61–64
consumer goods, 110, 131, 133
Council of Trent, 26, 163n17
Cronos (Saturn), 68
cross, 27–28, 151n64
crucifixion, 151n64
crucifixion scene, 28
Cupids (*Erotes*), winged, 69
curse, 21, 24, 53

d'Agoty, Jacques Fabien Gautier, 3, 67, 84, 125
death, 4, 19, 28, 39, 68, 70, 86–87, 143n10, 161n4, 163n21
de Gouges, Olympe, 61
Deimos (Metus), 70
de la Renta, Oscar, 170n7
Descartes, René, 46, 54
Descartes's cogito, 46
Dickson, Richard, 175–76
Diego, Saint Juan, 30
Diprose, Rosalyn, 148n50
discourse, 8, 59, 85, 87, 100

disjunction, 60, 108
divinity, 12, 14, 32, 63, 84, 105, 142n7
doctor, 33
Duncan, Byard, 158–59n45
duties, 137; childcare, 136; female, 54; male, 34, 36, 55; masculine, 40; professional, 157n30
Dworkin, Andrea, ix, 80, 140n2, 148–49n51, 163n20, 165n29, 166n37, 166n40

Eastern Orthodox communities, 26
Enlightenment, 45–46, 59, 61
Epstein, Jeffrey, 169n68
equality, 65, 133, 155n13; arguments for, 45; gender, 61; marriage, 145n25; -minded spouses, 52; woman's, 156n22
Ernst, Max, 28–30
Eros, 69
erotic love, 87
Estienne, Charles, 2–4
eternal life, 74
ethical values, 104
Euripides, 53, 159n52
evangelicalism, 145n24
Eve, 16–17, 20, 23, 32, 64, 145n26
existential: dread, 70; situation, 9; threat of death, 87; value, 42

fathers, cisgender, 136
Fausto-Sterling, Anne, 158n44

female: agency, 12–14, 27, 40, 43, 45, 73, 134; authority, 14, 59; body as sinful, 14; equality, 141n2; identity, liberal explorations of, 21; identity, logic of, 6; inequality, 8, 39; misogyny, 34; objectification, 104–5, 116, 123, 137, 141n2, 149n51, 169n68; personhood, reality of, 12; phenomenon, 14; politicians, intellectual, 45; postmodern identity, 135; rationality, 45, 47; subject, lived reality of, 132; subjectivity, logic of, 123; subjectivity, reimagination of, 91; subjects, mediation of, 10; subjugation, reality of, 155n13
females, 5, 44, 59, 153n1, 158n45
feminine: duties, 48; normative constraints on the, 28; norms, 41, 88, 97; order, Greek repression of, 59; order, logic of, 37; order, semiotic privileging of, 32; orders, 73–74, 87, 90; repression, 57; repression in religious practices, 57; strength, 30
femininity: and consumer forces, 137; cultural repression of, 55; instrumental use of, 107; normative performances of, 142n9; norms of, 83; orders of, 37
feminist: activism, 15; aestheticians, 176n38; body, interrogations of the, 6; call, 134; concern, 152n71; critiques, 10, 175n26; and educational opportunities for women, 63; erotic womb, engagement with, 88; goals of modern, 37; gospel, 123; and human nature, post-structural treatments of, 100; ideals, 61; imagination, 141n3; -informed phenomenology, 172n19; lens, 12; material womb, engagement with, 118; monotheistic, 168n67; phenomenologists, 148n50; philosophers, 173n19; philosophy, viii–ix, 7, 23; and pregnant subject, readings of the, 91; question, 8; readings, 22; resistance to oppression, xi; and sacred womb, engagement with, 30; suggestion, 81; teachers, 158n45; text, 155n18; theology, 140n1; views of author, 141n4; work, 56
fiction, 4, 8, 157n29
Fiore, Julia, 149n55
First Timothy 2:15, 22
flesh, 23, 60, 63, 66, 86, 121
Fletcher, Elizabeth, 151n68
Flusser, David, 144n15, 145n23
Fontana, Felice, 84–85
forbidden fruit, 20
Foucault, Michel, 147n40, 151n67, 165n34
Francis (pope), 23
freedom, xi, 8, 45, 55, 62, 90–91, 95, 102, 106, 122, 137, 140n8, 155n13, 156n29

Frey, Amanda, 147n41
Friedan, Betty, 54, 159n55

Gambero, Luigi, 144n16,
    145n26
Gandhi, Indira, 45, 157n30
Gatens, Moira, 148n50
Gaventa, Beverly Roberts, xii,
    143n11, 143n13, 144n14,
    144n16, 144nn20–22,
    147n42, 151–52n69,
    152nn70–71
gender: as fluid phenomenon,
    142n5; identity, xii, 52, 100,
    114, 172–73n19; normativ-
    ity, 131, 142n9; norms, 42,
    48, 50, 52, 102; performa-
    tivity, 79, 99, 101–2, 104;
    Western understanding of,
    160n78
Gibson, David, 149n54,
    151nn60–65, 160n72
God, 18, 30, 32, 150n58;
    children of, 12; and love of
    humanity, 63, 151n64; ordi-
    nation of marriage by, 14
goddesses, 38, 44, 58, 67,
    153nn1–2
gods, 36, 55, 59, 67, 69–70, 74
Gorgon, 49
Gospel of John, 16
Gospel of Luke, 16, 20,
    146n36
Gospel of Matthew, 16
Greek civic imagination, 44, 47
Greek mythology, 35, 126
Griffith, Donna, 141–42n4
Grosz, Elizabeth A., 141n4,
    148n50

Guenther, Lisa, 148n50
guilt, 52

Halberstam, Jack, x
halo, 28, 30
Hamilton, Mary, 7, 8, 140n4
Handler, Ruth, 93, 95, 101, 104,
    106, 174n25
Hansen, Danielle Tumminio, xii,
    158n42, 161–62n10
Harmonia (Concordia), 70
Harris, Kamala, 157n30
heartbeat bills, 32
Hegel, Georg Wilhelm Friedrich,
    173
Helen of Troy, 58
Hellenistic: examples, 77; peri-
    ods, 44
Hera, 58
Herakles, 57
Hermaphroditus, 73
Hermes, 58
Herodotus, 49
Hesiod, 153n1
heterosexual, 145n25
heuristics, 71
Hilton, Paris, 93
Hippolytus, 53
history, xii
Hofmeyr, Annelies, 116–17,
    176n38
holiness, 22
Holy Spirit, 16, 20, 23,
    63, 74
House of Venus in the Shell, 78
humanity, 12, 53, 90, 175n27

iconography, 24, 26, 72, 111,
    163n17

ideals, 95; archetypal, viii;
    civic, 36, 75; contradictory,
    80; cultural, 5; feminine,
    54; feminist, 61; gender,
    102; masculine, 37, 49–50;
    motherly, 12; mythic, 45;
    sociopolitical, 53;
    universal, 42; of woman-
    hood, 97
ideologies, 6, 10, 43, 125
imagination, 5; aesthetic, 77;
    Athenian civic, 153n1;
    cultural, 39, 47, 60, 83,
    161–62n10; Euro-
    American cultural and civic,
    157n30; feminist, 141n3;
    popular, 26
imaginings, 5, 11
Immaculate Conception,
    144n22
immanence, 12, 39–40, 42–43
impotence, 41, 155n18
individuals, 21, 71, 135, 173n19
infant, 32, 33, 74
injustice, 14
intellectual: activities, 24;
    exchange, xiii; freedom for
    women, 62
intelligence, 36, 157n31
intercourse, ix–x, 18, 68, 70, 78,
    82, 148n51
intersubjectivity, 82, 87,
    173–74n19
in vitro fertilization, 51
Irigaray, Luce, x, 158n38,
    177n42

Jenner, Caitlyn, 111
Jenner, Kris, 111

Jenner, Kylie, 111–12
Jesus, 8, 11, 15, 16, 19, 22, 24,
    27–28, 105, 124, 142n4,
    142–43n10, 149n55,
    150n48, 151n64, 151n69,
    152n71, 158n38
Jewish: faith, 20; feminist
    philosopher, ix;
    sources, 30
John Paul II, Saint (pope), 23
Johnson, Elizabeth A., 140n1,
    144n20
Joseph (husband of Mary), 28
Josiah, King, 144n17
joy, 27
judgment, 17, 24, 58, 81, 107

Kamitsuka, Margaret D.,
    146n30
Karimzadeh, Marc, 175–76n32
Kavilanz, Parija, 171n9
Ken (Barbie doll), 95, 131,
    171n9
Klaver, Elizabeth, 167n52,
    167–68n53, 168n54
knowledge, x, 27
Kolb, Steven, 175n32
Korsmeyer, Carolyn, 141n4
Kotz, Liz, 171nn12–13,
    172n18

labor pains, 38
Lang, Justin, 144n15, 145n23
Laqueur, Thomas, 153n1,
    154n10, 159nn56–60,
    159nn67–68,
    160nn69–70
Law of Deuteronomy, 144n17
Lennox, Annie, 93

Leopold II, 84

LGBTQIA+, 102, 176n37

Libya, ancient, 49

Llywelyn, Dorian, 142n8,
147n43, 147nn45–46,
148n48, 151n66,
153n78

logic, 60, 108, 142n7

Loraux, Nicole, 153n1,
154nn7–8, 155n17,
156n26, 156n28,
159nn48–52,
159nn65–66

Lorde, Audre, 156n22

Loukas, Marios, 168n55

love, 22, 133, 150n58; Aphrodite, goddess of, 58; father's
self, 163n21; goddess, 74,
77, 84, 87, 127; God's,
female symbol of, 24; God's,
for humanity, 63, 151n64;
-mate on the half shell, 68;
Roman goddess of, 68; sex
and, 69; sexuality and, 87;
and submission, 147n38

Mackie, Bob, 175n32

Macrone, Michael, 161nn4–5

Madonna with the Long Neck, 29

make-believe, 94, 103, 110, 112,
131, 169n1, 174–75n26

male: agency, 19; authority,
136; civic engagement, 44;
dominance, 71; norms of
desirability, 81, 90; religious
transcendence, 83; strength,
49

man, 13, 51, 78, 122,
158–59n45, 163nn20–21;

feminine, 154n10; feminine,
reality of a, 154n10; as gender category, 100; ideal, 98;
mythic superiority of, 54

Man, 46

Maria lactans (the nursing
Madonna), 24, 26, 63,
150n58

Marian, 80: activities, 76, 129,
133; apparitions, 152n72;
archetype, 12, 21, 153n76;
-Athenian focus, 75; authority, 29; -Christian scheme,
21; concepts, 17, 126;
constructions, 27; example,
70; iconography, 72; names,
images, and associations,
16; theology, 22; vehicle,
83; womanhood, ideology
of, 126

"Marienleben," 150n58

Mariology, 143n10, 152n71;
christotypical, 22, 30; and
economic authority, 33;
modern, 33

marital relationships, 21

marriage, 56, 104, 154n9;
avoiding, 103; Barbie and,
95, 98–100; bounds of, 17;
fruitfulness in, 22; by God,
14; Hera, goddess of, 58;
heterosexual, 18, 142n7;
and Mary, 143n13; same-
sex, 142n7, 145n25; sex
and, 145nn24–25; Venus
and, 69

Marshall, Helen, 141n4,
146n31

Martin, Emily, 166–67n39

Mary: and agency, 23, 63, 143n10, 152n71; as agential, 17, 26; and agential identities, 33; and agential mothering, 24; as agential woman, 30; as agential womb, 22; as archetype, 7, 12, 19, 137, 149n51, 171n10; and assisted reproductive technologies (ART), 145n25; and Athena, 63–65, 69–70, 133; and authority, 143n10; and Barbie, 95–96, 98, 105–7, 131–32, 174n22, 174–75n26, 175n27; and Beyoncé, 30–32; biblical, 8; and biblical details of, 105; body, disclosure of as spiritual force, 134; and children, 151–52n69; choice of maternity of, 24; in Christian art, 149nn54–55, 150–51n58, 151nn60–65; and christotypical Mariology, 22–23; christotypical readings of, 45; and civic ideals, 75; confessional reading of, 141n4; as container, figurative, 16, 124; and dolls, 174n22; elevation to holiness of, 145n23; eroticism of, 73; as eternal figure, 16; Eve, contrast with, 20; exemplar of fertility, 33; family history of, 105; and female agency, 133; feminist readings of, 141–42n4, 152n71; holiness of, 24; humble Jewish woman, 16; impregnated by Holy Spirit, 143n13, 145n25; Jewish mother of Jesus, 15, 124; as Maryam, 16; material work of, 160n71; maternity of, 20, 91; as mother, figurative, 19; and motherhood, 20–21; as mother of God, 33; as nonagential subject, 75; ontological status of, 161n10; and ontological tensions, 15; as Other, 12; as passive vessel, 15–21; and performance of feminine subjectivity, 33; and performance of motherhood, 19; and performance of pregnancy, 8, 11, 14–15, 27, 69, 132; and performance of womanhood, 15, 30; personal history of, 15; purity of, 151n58; as queen of heaven, 33; rational assent of, 23, 63; readings of, 142–43n10, 143n143, 144nn14–20, 146nn32–37, 175n29; reimagination of, 143n10; and relationship with God, 16–18, 21–23, 25, 27, 63; relationship to the masculine, 37; religious emphasis on, 22; and religious services, attendance of, 28; in the Roman Catholic tradition, 145n25; as saint, 16; as saint of motherhood, 33; as servant, 16; as sister, 33; and spiritual authority, 25, 28; as spiritual mother,

24–26, 33; stripped of
rationality, 23; submission to
authority of, 30; as teacher,
16; theological interpretation
of seduction of, 143n10;
and Venus, 74–76, 81, 83,
127, 161–62n10, 163n22;
virginity of, 17, 19, 35, 70,
144n22, 145n23, 145n26;
and wisdom, inspiration of,
25; as woman, 27–30; and
womanhood, 8; and womb,
5, 9, 33, 40, 152n73; and
womb as sacred space, 11,
13–14, 18, 24, 74, 124–25;
as young Jewish virgin, 20
masculine: coding of women, 41;
duties, 48, 52; norms, 37,
98; norms of womanhood,
82; orders, 73–74, 87, 90
mass communication, 26
maternity, 16, 19, 20–21, 123,
147n40, 149n52; leave, 62;
and power, 91
Mattel, 96–98, 105–7, 109, 112,
122; modeled-by-, 176n37;
Toy Company, 94, 105; Toy
Factory, 104
Mattel, Trixie, 114–15
Max, Peter, 170n7
Mayerson, Philip, 154n3
medical: advances, 62; detection
of fetal heartbeat, 32; doctor,
106, 106; forces, 134;
literature, 146n31; reform,
5; school, 84, 127; students,
1; study, 26–27; understanding, 4
Meir, Golda, 45, 157n30

men: heterosexual, 136, 164n23,
177n5; intellectual activity
of, 55; as rational, 55
menstruation, 50
Merleau-Ponty, Maurice, 173
Messiah, 8
Metis (wife of Zeus), 38, 40,
153–54n2
Metus (Deimos), 70
Mexico, 30
Midge (Barbie doll), 119,
130–31
Miles, Margaret R., 151n64,
163n17
miracles, 26, 32
misogyny, 39, 54, 100, 153n1
modern technology, 5
Moffett, Chris, 155n16
money, 4, 8, 50, 56, 105–6, 136,
166n37, 175n27; counter-
feit, 53
motherhood: agential forms of,
15; normative division of,
76, 90
Mullin, Amy, x, 153n77, 167n44
Mulvey, Laura, 165n33
Murphy, Francesca A.,
146nn32–35, 148n47,
148n49, 149n52

narrative, 150n58
narrator, 8, 18
neoclassical art, 3
neoclassicism, 77
new Eve, 16, 32
New Testament, 15, 143n10
Nietzsche, Friedrich, 35
Nietzschean, 48
nonbinary subject positions, 76

normative, 172n19; compliance,
14; equivalency, 12; femininity, 110; gender expectations, 40; practices, 41, 134,
147n40, 165n34; successes
and failures, 129; view, 22;
ways, 157n30
norms, 109; bodily, 131; female,
54, 136; female bodily, 57;
of female embodiment,
113; feminine, ordained by
God, 21; ideologies and, 10;
market, 131; sexist, viii; of
womanhood, 9
nudity, 26, 150n8
Nursing Madonna, The, 24–25

Obergefell v. Hodges, 145n25
objectification, process of, 108
obstetrics, 64, 87
Old Testament, ix, 64, 144n17
Oliver, Kelly, x, 166n38, 167n40
ontological boundaries, 116
ontological category, 59
ontological difference, 162n10
ontological questions, 176n33
Orthodox theologians, 144n22
Ouranos (Uranus or Caelus), 68
Our Lady of Guadalupe, 30,
152n72
Ovid, 58

pain, 72, 78–79, 88
Panathenaic prize, 48
Pandora, 153n1
Paris, Ginette, 160n2, 161n4,
161n8, 163nn15–16,
163nn18–19, 167nn45–46,
168n67

Parmigianino, 28–29
patriarchy, 9, 162n10, 166n35
Paul VI (pope), 22, 147n
Pelikan, Jaroslav, 144n15,
145n23, 146n37, 147n39
Peloponnesian War, 44
performativity, 97, 101–2, 135
Persaud, T. V. N., 168nn55–56
personhood: conditions for, 41;
female, 12; performance of,
13; psychic structures of, 80;
wombed, 71, 90, 110
phenomenological: accounts,
172n19; insights, 141n2;
readings of feminists, 141n4;
task, 173n19
phenomenology: feminist-
informed, 172n19; material,
148n50; of miscarriage, vii;
of pregnancy, 19; of pregnant embodiment, 166n38;
traditional, 173n19; of
transcendence, 65
philosophy, xiv; Cartesian, 54;
feminist, viii, 7, 23,
141n4; history of, 6; language of, ix
Phobos (Timor), 70
Phrynos, 38
physicians, 9, 74, 84
polis, 40, 56, 65, 160n78
Pooler, David K., 147n41
pornographic materials,
163n17
pornographic views, 79
pornography, 26
postmodern pastiche, 118
pregnancies, figurative, 24, 77,
149n53

pregnancy: as agential phenomenon, 14; as ambiguous phenomenon, 134; as intellectual
productivity, 82; and patriarchy, 134; phenomenological
fluidity of, 146n31; phenomenological richness of, 23; as
physical phenomenon, 23; as
self-affirming phenomenon,
123; sorrow of, 27
pregnant: bodies, reimagination
of, 30; subjectivity, reimagination of, 15
priest, 33
printing press, 26
pro-life narrative, 146n30
Prometheus, 38, 153–54n2
prophet, 16, 33
prophetic knowing, 27
prophetic practices, 22
Protestantism, 26
Protestants, 14, 16, 17, 18, 22,
141n4, 145n24, 152–53n74
Protoevangelium of James,
144n22, 145n23
providence, 26
Psalms, 18–19
Pseudo-Apollodorus, 38, 153n2
psychological: attachments, 70;
forces, 134; function, 71;
imperatives, 158n45; move,
106; role, 143n11; tensions,
15; well-being, 166n37
public-private distinction, 47
purity, 23, 33, 143n10; movements, 17; sacred, 144n22,
145n23

Qur'an, 16

race, human, 20, 145n26
rape, 88, 143n10
rational: act, 36; activities, 18;
agent, 13; capacity, 2, 9, 64;
individual subjects, 109;
thought, 62
rationality, 156n22; articulations
of, 46; lack of male, 155n19;
of men, 55
reality, 46, 86; of human difference, 108; male experiences
of, ix; material, 49; representation of, 111; troubling, 5;
understanding of, 167n47
Realy, Margaret Rose,
150nn56–57, 151n59
religious: iconography, 24; relationships, 21; subjects, 26
Richmann, Christopher, xiii,
152n74, 153n76
ritual, 33
Roberts, Barbara Millicent (Barbie), 94
Roman Catholic, 16, 18, 141n4,
145n24, 146n30; circles, and
contemporary purity move-
ments within, 17; devotion,
Lady of Guadalupe as symbol
of, 30; espousal of chastity,
14; feminist theological perspective, 140n1; and repression of female authority, 14;
stance on marriage, 145n24
Roman Catholic Church, 22
Roman Empire, 27
Romans, 68
Rubin, Miri, 150n58, 160n71
Ruether, Rosemary Radford,
142–43n10, 152n71

RuPaul, 114
Ryan (Barbie doll), 131

salvation, 18–20, 24, 26,
    175n27; history of, 19
Sartre, Jean-Paul, 172n19
Saturn (Cronus or Cronos), 68,
    72, 163n21
Schaberg, Jane, 142–43n10, 152n71
Schiebinger, Londa, 156n19,
    157n31, 159n53,
    160nn73–74, 171n9
Schultz, Anne-Marie, xi, 154n11
Scripture, 15, 18, 26, 144n17,
    153n74
Seaton, Mary, 8, 140n4
self, agential, 8
self, reimagination of, 71
self-identity, 6, 9, 13, 18–19,
    110, 122, 136, 169n1
Semonides, 53
servant leadership, 20
sex, 39, 44, 66, 68–71, 84; the act
    itself, 78; appeal, of Venus,
    75; Athena's, 55; binary, 99;
    civilizing function of, 90; as
    duly sacred, 80; female, 83;
    flesh, 60; male, 57; male-
    female construction of, 100;
    -positive feminists, 80; power
    of, 74; resignification of, 91;
    spiritual and civic functions
    of, 79; transfigured represen-
    tations of, 82; and Venus, 76
sex doll, 104
sexual: coding of women, 91;
    desire, 27, 36, 70, 78, 81,
    91, 101, 104; gratification,
    ix, 13, 60, 148n51

sexuality: Greek, 57; heteronor-
    mative, 91
Seyffert, Oskar, 160nn1–2,
    161n7
Shakespeare, William, 140n8,
    156–57n29
shame, 104, 177n2
Simmons, Laurie, 174n23
sinners, 17, 24, 26, 64, 150n58
siren, 49
sister, 157n29
Sleeping Venus, 87
social media, 32
social orders, 79, 83
sonogram, 33
Southern Baptist Convention,
    146–47n38
Spretnak, Charlene, 161n8
strength, 157n31, 168n67
Suarez, Francisco, 148n49
Suarezian, 149n52
Susini, Clemente, 86, 127–28,
    168n59
Swedlund, Alan C., 171n9,
    171n11, 175n28,
    175nn30–31,
    176nn34–37

technicians, 9
Tegner, Rudolph, 126
Thatcher, Margaret, 45, 157n30
theological: imaginings, 11, 15;
    meanings, 104
theology, 143n10
theology, Christian, 16
Theotokos (God-bearer), 16
Thespius, 57
Timor (Phobos), 70
Titian, 77

transcendence, 42, 44, 104, 122, 133, 160n77; of body, 65; from despair, 70; male religious, 83; miraculous, 12; as an organizing principle, 39; sexual, 79
trans women, 135, 142n6
Trinity, the, 25
Trojan War, 59
Trophy Wife Barbie, 116–17, 176n38, 177n39
Troy, fall of, 69
Tubbs, R. Shane, 168n55
Tucker, Jason, 153n75

ultrasound, 32
Uranus, 68
Urla, Jacqueline, 171n9, 171n11, 175n28, 175nn30–31, 176nn34–37
uterus, 4, 9, 38, 54, 83, 119

Venerina (little Venus), 86, 127–28
Venus: aesthetic appeal of, 68; aesthetic power of, 79; and agency, 76, 83, 90; as agential subject, 88, 90–91, 133; as alluring goddess, 75, 132; as anatomical model, 84–88; as androgynous womb, 74–77; as archetype, 49, 79, 129, 137; in art, 77–78, 84; and Athena, 127, 133, 163nn21–22; and authority, 79; and Barbie, 95–96, 98, 131–32; and civic functions, 79; and civic order, 96; as civilizing force, 68–74; creation account of, 67–68, 71–74, 162n14, 163n18; cultural power of, 105–6; as doll, 84, 127; eroticization of motherhood and, 81, 83; and female agency, 75, 77; Italian goddess of spring, 67; as love goddess, 74, 77, 84; luxurious hair of, 102; and Mary, 127, 133, 161–62n10, 163n22; ontology of, 84; other names of, 161n7; and paradigm of womanhood, 82; performance of pregnancy, 69–70, 75, 91, 132; popular appeal of, 133; and pregnancy, 79, 83; and pregnancy, religious meaning of, 76, 133; relationship to the masculine, 37, 76, 80, 133; relationship to motherhood, 76; religious value of, 106; as Roman goddess of love, 68, 127; saving intimacy, 134; as sex goddess, 68; and sexual arousal as religious ecstasy, 70; and sexual desire, 70, 161n5; as sexual icon, 77–82; and sexuality, 163n20; and sexual norms, 162n13; and spiritual elevation of sex, 162n11; and subdual of man, 74; as tainted womb, 82–84; as *Venus Genetrix*, 69; as *Venus Verticordia*, 69; as *Venus Victrix*, 69; of Willendorf, 156n21; as woman, 84–88; and womb, 9; and womb as erotic space, 5, 66, 77, 89–90

Venus Anadyomeme, 78
Venus de' Medici, 77
Venus of Urbino, 77
Vesalius, Andreas, 85
Vintges, Karen, 172–73n19
Virasana, 32
Virgin of Guadalupe, 30, 152n72
virtue, 17, 164n27
vita activa, 46

walnut seed, 24–25
Walton, Kendall L., 169n1, 170n6
Warhol, Andy, 170n7
Warren, Elizabeth, 45, 157n30
Weaver, Douglas (Doug), xii, 145n24, 152n74
Weinstein, Harvey, 169n68
Wendell, Susan, 160n77
Werner the Swiss, 150n58
Western: cultural imagination, 83; culture, 57; disease, 85; empires, 64; tradition, 46, 56; world, 11, 127
Williams, Florence, 163n17
Williamson, Sarah, 117, 177n40
wisdom, 66, 157n36
Wollstonecraft, Mary, 61, 80, 140n2, 154n10, 155n18, 159n47, 164n27
woman, 4, 16, 123–24, 140n8, 145n23, 151n67, 157n29, 158n39, 171n13, 174n26; and agency, 88; as animal trophy, 116; archetypes of, 132, 134; from Athens, 156n26; and authority, 88, 122; becoming a, xi, 47, 135; being a, 50; being born a, 83; casting oneself as, 96, 132; as commodity, 106–7; concept of, 139n3, 140n2, 153n1; contemporary critique of, 131; deceased, 86; delivered, 32; desirous, 80; as doll, 112; as empty category, 65; erasure of, 19; essence of, 13; essentialist constructions of, 123; as evil, 84; experiencing oneself as a, viii; as feminine object, 15; ideal, 171n10; laboring as a, 46–47; live, think, and act as, 10; Mary's model of, 15; as masculine, 42, 52, 142n9, 154n10, 155n18, 159n47; as mother, 1, 97; as narrative construction, 6, 124; new performances of, x; as object, 171n14; as object of beauty, 141n2; as Other, 140n2, 164n28; performance of, 21, 123, 162n10; postmenopausal, 51; and pregnancy, 7, 90; pregnant, 19; and the *Qur'an*, 16; as a reproductive creature, 43; as sacred vessel, 133; sexual, suspension of, 161n9; and sexual allure, 166n35; subjects, subordination of, 81; as toy, 106; as trickster, 114; Wollstonecraft's views on, 164n27; and womb, 9–13, 18, 109, 122; as womb, 5, 14, 17, 21–22, 28, 43, 95, 97, 100, 103, 123, 126, 173n19; Woolfian exploration of, 4; as worldly, 17

womanhood: ideals of, 97; imaginings of, 71, 162n10; logic of, viii; narrative sign of, 124; normative, 97, 98

woman's: embodied agency, 22; history, 156n19; Otherness, viii, 80; power, paradoxical logic of, 23; self-identity, 41

womb, xi, 1, 4–5, 33, 100, 134, 141n3, 169n68, 171n10; acquisition of goodness and, 23; activity of the, 62; as androgynous, 74; and authority, ix, 90; biological, refusal of the, 44; biological signification of, 136; body as, 19; coding of, 125; as condition of womanhood, 49; cultural suppression of the, 40; as divine, 18; as divine space, 152–53n74; embodied, 155n13; erotic, 77, 88, 90; erotic coding of, 68; as erotic space, 66–67, 76, 133, 135; female, 39; and female experience, 7; female sex as a, 122; as female space, 71; and female subjectivity, 110; fertile, 96; a fetus growing in the, 124; goodness in her, 148n49; hegemony of the, 91; Holy Spirit and, 16, 20; identifying woman with a, 13; identity with a, viii; imaginings of the, 15; as immaterial, 38; impregnated, 9, 123; inert, 164n28; legacy of the, 59; liquid, 73; as material, 118; as material space, 93, 99, 129, 131, 135; mind as, 47; mother's, 164n25; performance of woman as, 21; as political space, 34–36, 41, 61, 63, 135; politics of the, 158n41; readings of the, 123; reimagination of, 27; religious significance of, 60; reproductive, 101; as sacred, 30; as sacred space, 11, 24, 75, 132, 135, 142n7, 152n73, 153n76; as self-producing, 142n5; as semiotic organ, 142n5; source of female power, 32; as source of knowledge, 27; suspension of, 56; as tainted, 84; as therapeutic device, 71; as unfeminine, 43; woman as, 14, 17, 21, 28, 95, 97, 100, 103, 123, 126, 173n19; woman is but a, 22; woman not just a, 12; woman with a, 10; as zone of male entry, 82

women: and access to religious activities, 56; and agency, 5, 10, 39–40, 142n9, 154n4; as agential subjects, ix; American, 45; ancient, in religious roles, 57; and authority, 5, 39, 50, 71, 82, 142n10; customary duties of, 27; and domestic duties, the performance of, 42; as figurative warriors, 49; Greek, religious roles of, 44; and integrity, 148n51;

women (*continued*): and intellectual labor, 90, 141n3; as irrational, 55; man-hating, 95; metaphoric productivity of, 136; metaphysical impoverishment of, 92; objectification of, 68, 117, 164n28; rational capacities of, 54, 62; as rational creatures, 61; rationality of, 61; as rational professionals, 157n30; reality of, 156n29; sexual objectification of, 116, 166n35; subverting patriarchy, 71

women's: agency, 15, 34, 123, 141n4; agential status, 142n9; authority, 141n4; equality, xii, 40, 60; identity as Other, 135; inequality, 34, 61; intellectual interests, 54; limited agency, 100; sexual oppression, rejection of, 83

Woolf, Virginia, ix, 4, 7–8, 37, 121–22, 136, 139nn1–2, 139–40n4, 140nn5–8, 155nn13–14, 156n29, 157n, 166n37, 177n1, 177nn6–7

Woolfian, 4, 133, 136

Wright, Henry, xiv, 108, 130

Wright, J. Lenore, 169n1, 170nn5–6, 172n17, 174nn20–21

Young, Iris Marion, x, 166n38, 169n68

Young Virgin Spanking the Infant Jesus in Front of Three Witnesses, 28

Zeus, 35, 38–40, 53, 58, 81, 153–54n2, 155n16, 161n4, 163n18, 174n25

Ziegfeld, Florenz, 165n33